A love
less ordinary

Laura Newman

BRAMLEY

PRESS

Published in Great Britain by Bramley Press
www.bramleypress.co.uk

Copyright © 2012 Laura Newman

The moral right of the author has been asserted.

www.angelandprincess.wordpress.com

A CIP catalogue record for this book is available from the British Library.

ISBN 978-0-9571325-2-8

Acknowledgements

I would not be where I am without having had the strength, support and love from my beautiful and amazing Nicci.

I am blessed with close friends and family who are incredibly warm-hearted and giving, without whose love and acceptance life would not be so fulfilling.

I would like to thank the many organisations who showed belief that there was an interest in this project, with a special mention to TransPartners.co.uk and GIRES, and to all the readers of my blog.

To my friends who identify as transgender; it is an honour to know you and be inspired by you all.

Thanks to all those who put their heart on their sleeve and agreed to be interviewed for this book, and all those who have touched me along this journey.

Contents

Prologue	1
Wake up	5
Revelations	14
What a Difference a T Makes	21
An Ideal Relationship?	26
Rules of Attraction	35
The L Word	43
If It's Not a Personal Question	52
Man, I Feel Like a Woman!	57
The Pronoun Game	66
Gender Bending	71
Social Order	78
Natural vs Normal	84
(S)expectations	92
A Touchy Subject	101
The Pitfalls	110
A Class Act	119
Who Am I, if He Becomes She?	126
Understanding, Acceptance, Integration	131
Shout it From the Rooftops!	139
A Better Life	148
Appendix: Here comes the science bit …	155

Don't walk behind me, I may not lead.
Don't walk in front of me, I may not follow.
Just walk beside me and be my friend.

Albert Camus

Prologue

ou can live a better life, not by owning possessions and being driven by material aspirations, but by the decisions you make of how to live your life. Many of us like to think we make these decisions regularly, that we have strength of character to some degree, and some spark of uniqueness and individuality that sets us apart from others. But have you ever woken up one day and found yourself wondering: 'What happened to me? Where is the me I once was? Something feels out of kilter—I am sure that this is not who I was meant to be.' When I experienced this for myself, it felt as though I had let all the mundane aspects of life strip me, reduce me and rob from me, until I had become an empty shell of titles—nothing more than a number of little boxes to tick. Daughter, sister, boss, girlfriend; delete as applicable. It was as though I had spent most of my life wading through treacle, existing—not living, just existing—day to day as a messy bundle of others' expectations.

If pushed to really think about these issues, you might come to the conclusion that, at some point in your life's journey, you have fallen asleep at the wheel. If forced to be honest, I think the majority of us would have to admit that we have forgotten (or maybe never learnt) what it is to fully live and love life every single day, for every beautiful moment of it; drinking in all the simple pleasures that life brings. It is not just about setting a goal and obtaining it. It is the journey that counts.

I fell into this trap: I clawed my way out. I fell into all of the above traps and arrived at a point where I said: 'No more. I deserve respect, genuine love and fulfilment of my dreams.' I gave myself the greatest gift any of us can give ourselves; I gave myself the gift of choice.

So many of us get into this situation; we wade through our daily lives, never noticing or questioning the way we are living them. We compromise. We learn to satisfy others' needs over our own. We behave how others want and live by the rules that society has set for each of our separate roles. We act as good little citizens and family members, and in the thick of it all we lose the most important person in the world: ourselves. If a tragedy strikes—perhaps a death, the loss of job or a home—we pick ourselves up and get on with it. How many of us stop to ask: 'what would I sacrifice my world for—what would I give my life for?' It is hard to decide whether we should throw everything away and start again or merely salvage what we have left. Everybody fears this choice. Risk is something many of us avoid, partly because we are crippled by fear and partly because we settle for 'good'. If we have a 'good' life, it may be that we don't feel it is necessary to rock the boat. We settle for 'good' rather than reaching for 'great'.

Whether or not we accept this as fact, we all need human kindness. Although animals need comfort of a sort, what sets us apart from them is the degree to which we need it.

In our search for companionship, we compromise ourselves because we fear that others may not like our true selves. We hide away, selecting which parts of ourselves to show others, leading us to show only the traits we think are our most likable. So it is little wonder that so many relationships break down; not just romantic relationships, but relationships with friends and family. And if you suppress something for long enough, eventually it will erupt. An example is an argument. Remember a row that you have had with someone and how often it is about something trivial, completely blown out of proportion. Something has festered, eating away at you both until part of you rots and breaks, crumbling to pieces.

As women, we hope and dream that we can find that special someone; Mr Right, with whom we can happily share our lives. Obviously, it will all be perfect, and outbursts of a distasteful nature will not occur because there is a shared understanding between you both. But in searching for Mr Right, we set the bar at its highest point. We look for perfection, as though we have an idealist's shopping list of expectations to be fulfilled. For our part, if we can hide all the aspects of ourselves we are not happy with, Mr Right will stay with us and we will walk off into the sunset to live happily ever after. But there is a flaw in this way of thinking. Anything worth preserving, including relationships, takes time and effort to keep going.

The truth is, Mr Right only exists to those who have accepted themselves. Over everything else, you must love yourself and consider You to be the most important person in your life. This cannot be compromised. You must love You. You must accept You. You must respect, honour and treasure You.

I hope that in writing this book, I may inspire someone—if only one person—to find the bravery to challenge their life; to read this and ask themselves the same questions I did. Though uncomfortable, I think it is necessary. Every now and then, I still ask myself these questions. I review my life and ask myself: 'Am I still happy with my life? Am I doing what is making me happy? Is the relationship I am in causing me to lose myself?'

If you ask yourself these questions and more importantly, do something about the answers, you are less likely to come to a point in your future where it all goes wrong and you cannot fathom why; you do not know where you took a wrong turn and came across a dead end.

The heart and essence of this book is about more than merely me in an alternative type of relationship—all relationships have their own unique elements and can be equally wonderful. It is about learning to love yourself—learning to live the life that you want and be truly free as the person you were meant to be. Someone like my partner, with all the challenges she faces, can do this; so couldn't we all find the courage to be honest about our real selves? Having woken up and realised that I was not living life the way I should have been, I have gained great perspective of what a fulfilling, healthy relationship can be; and what it should be.

It is my wish to help people become aware, understand, accept and be tolerant of different kinds of relationships and the individuals involved in them. By doing so, I hope to make coming out easier for them and their partners; to let them be accepted, as the gay movement has made homosexuality so widely accepted. There are too many people out there who are still hiding from themselves in fear.

I would like to share my experience with you; the story of what makes a good relationship—with a twist. I want to dispel the myths that the media portrays, and I would love for other women out there to be open minded in considering the possible benefits of a love less ordinary.

Wake up

B
efore I begin to expand on my current relationship, I feel I should first outline my relationship background. I feel that it is important to note that I have had my fair share of real relationship experience—the good and the bad.

For thirteen years, I had been in a relationship with someone who I thought was 'The One'—my then partner, who will be known as 'H' from here on in. The Hallmark/Hollywood condition for a romantic love story is that you would do anything for the other person; you would move heaven and earth and you would die for them. This, however, opens up the relationship to total dependency. Trying to help H had suffocated my true personality, as much as if I had placed the pillow over my own face and gently started to apply pressure.

Running around after someone else, attending to their every need and making sure their wants are met is exhausting and unsustainable—most of all, I think it is damaging to the relationship and more importantly, damaging to you. Eventually you will burn out and this is where resentment starts to creep in, like a virus that first eats away at the fabric of your union. Then, if you are lucky enough to have spotted the signs, you will realise that it has also eaten away at you as an individual and you have deviated from your chosen path in life. Perversely, by not taking care of your needs, your partner cannot enjoy the company of a full and well-rounded version of you—the person you really are.

There were many signs that something wasn't right between H and me. I had an uncomfortable, niggling feeling that resurfaced every few years. I had been going it alone more and more; I had grown and developed but my partner was standing still. I kept looking back, waiting for him to catch up, but he wasn't willing. He kept standing there, looking at me, like his feet were stuck in the mud. It was frustrating and painful. Why couldn't he follow me, if he loved me? All this is in retrospect, of course—wonderful, yet useless. Back then, I must have subconsciously recognised that I could not develop further as an individual if I let him hold me back. So I carried on forward, gaining momentum while he became scenery, finally becoming no more than a pin point on the landscape.

With the break-up of any relationship, it is difficult to pinpoint the time, place or reason; perhaps there was that one thing that you read, or something someone said to you, which gave you some crashing realisation that your relationship was on the rocks. For me it was more like the dripping of a tap. I know that towards the end of our relationship, other areas of my life were also seriously out of kilter, such as my job, which was unsteady and in a state of fragile change. Success in my career had always been my source of strength and confidence; it made me very stressed and I started losing a worrying amount of weight.

I remember that an awakening had started to creep up on me; in being with H, I had lost who I was and I started to wonder who I could be on my own. I imagined what kind of life I could have without him in it. These were very guilty thoughts at first, but I slowly learned to place myself in higher priority than him, for the first time ever.

Though mainly a slow corrosion, there were moments of our relationship that I realised were so destructive to me, they sent chills down my spine. I am reticent about giving an example to help illustrate this, as I am ashamed—ashamed of some of the things I agreed to do in order to maintain peace and to keep H happy at all costs. Nevertheless, I realise you may struggle to understand the footing the relationship was on, so I will put my heart on my sleeve and lose the fear, and share an example that might help you understand.

H and I did not live together. For some people that is shocking enough, considering we were together for so many years. This was for several reasons, most (if not all) of which I have now come to realise were only excuses that I bought into, and unwittingly perpetuated.

One of the more honourable reasons was that H was living at his parents' house, initially to help his mother nurse his father who had suffered from a stroke; after which the reason became to nurse his mother, who was dying of cancer. Later on, H gave several 'reasons' as to why, after his mother passed away, I could not move in with him temporarily until we finally bought our own place together. H was sleeping in his childhood bedroom in a single bed—by then his father was in a home, and before his mother had died she had been forced to swap the marital bed for a medical bed. As a result, at weekends when I would stay at the house, there was only his single bed for us to sleep in.

There were countless solutions to this (particularly as money was not an issue for him) but also an equivalent quantity of excuses. His argument was that he needed a good night's sleep at weekends, as he was often tired from his job. He did not want to share his single bed, which we would not both fit into comfortably enough, because then he would not have the good night's sleep he required. Instead, I ended up with a poor night's sleep every weekend, on an uncomfortable camp bed set up at the side of his bed. It is tragically humiliating that I allowed, worse, agreed, to this over a long period of time.

I would insist on lying in H's bed with him for a hug before being relegated to the camp bed. Even then, he couldn't wait to get rid of me, to have his precious night's sleep, while I tossed and turned and had yet another weekend's sleepless night. On one occasion, when I expressed that I was unhappy with this arrangement, he said bluntly: 'You know where the door is.' I did indeed, but I reasoned on that particular occasion that I had drunk some wine and so couldn't drive myself home. So I didn't leave; I slunk off to that camp bed.

In a later argument, when I had found some strength from the mouse I had become, I took great satisfaction in telling him that he could 'burn the bloody camp bed' as far as I was concerned.

It took some time to realise that a person who genuinely loved and respected me (and was of a healthy mind) would not act this way, and that I was not being the strong, confident, intelligent woman I knew myself to be. How could I, when this was what I was allowing to happen behind closed doors? Clearly I had very little self-respect to be in such a passively destructive relationship.

Our relationship had ceased to be physical—not only was it not sexual, but it also lacked a level of physical intimacy one might expect from a couple. I certainly still cared about his welfare but these feelings had become platonic and this was part of my decision to end the relationship. I knew I had to do what was the right thing for me but I was battling with not wanting to hurt him just for the sake of untangling myself. At some point I acknowledged that it was a necessary evil, for the purpose of self-preservation.

On reflection, he spent the whole of our relationship pushing me away in several subtly insensitive ways. He was very uncomfortable with any displays of emotion; he hated me crying because it served 'no purpose'. Well, of course it serves little purpose in actually resolving whatever it is you are crying about—but indulging in a weeping session can make you feel a hell of a lot better!

Besides, it's an emotional reaction. You can't control it. I did try to control it, on many occasions, in order not to upset him. When I think back on this, I feel as though I am looking on the memory as if it were a scene in a play. I am a character, a shadow of myself, but certainly not me. How deeply tragic and disturbing it is that a human being would try and stifle a natural act such as crying in what is supposed to be a loving relationship, simply because she knows that it makes the other person uncomfortable! If you are upset to the point of needing to cry and it gives the other person discomfort, they should be the one dealing with their discomfort, not you. You are obviously already trying to deal with something difficult—ideally, the other person should be helping you with that.

H said that all his other partners had left him in the end. It seemed I had simply been the stupid one who had put up with it for much longer than the others. I had taken longer to get the hint that he wasn't really built for an adult, sexual relationship. Whether or not any part of me thought that I could change him, I'm not sure. Here lies the problem with relationships; either we think we can change the other person or, without realising it, we get changed through the years of the relationship. It takes a conscious effort to remain your own person.

When faced with a rocky patch in their relationship, some may decide to stay and work things out. They may be willing to forgive and forget. That might be absolutely the right thing for that particular relationship. At the point when I told H it was all over, he reeled off a list of all the things he knew he should and shouldn't have done and everything he would change if I stayed. He was virtually on his knees begging me to stay, making promises which just felt empty and reeked of desperation. He was throwing all the ammunition he had in the battle, fighting back desperately—but then again, there is no reason why he should have made it easy for me.

Yet in some ways, his reaction really did make my decision easier. He had known, all those years, that he was taking me for granted; he was telling me to my face, in so many words, that he knew; yet, he had been complacent in making attempts to repair our situation beforehand. Once the confession started, it flowed like a torrid, ugly shower. Honestly, after all his words, which filled me with so much hurt, resentment and anger at him—not to mention at myself, for putting up with it for so long and not seeing the truth sooner—how could I have continued to be involved with him?

He must have known his failures all along and knowingly declined to make any effort to change. For him to confess all that he knew was wrong, as he did when I was ending the relationship, meant he knew—

he knew—what was happening, but it suited him just fine to continue as we were, as it meant he didn't have to make any special effort.

When push came to shove, I'd had enough. I had too much resentment that he had not put the same amount of effort into the relationship as I had. I couldn't help but feel that he wanted this; that he wanted to hit rock bottom, so he could truly wallow and complain that he had gone through tough times. The scary thing is, he nearly pulled me down with him.

So really and truly, how could I ever have made things work from such a low point? At the very least, the emphasis was on I not he. From my position of anger, I felt a sudden yearning for all the things I'd missed in catering for H's needs. In this way, he was the one who essentially drove me into the arms of someone else.

I saw that it was not just my individuality that I was denying when I was with H. I was also denying myself the opportunity to be in a relationship that suited my needs; for all those years, my full focus had been in trying to make another person happy and I was beginning to see a possibility of something more reciprocal.

Up until that point, starting a new relationship was not an option in my mind. I could not consider it. I owed it to our relationship to try and work things out between us, once I had acknowledged the things that were lacking, I owed it to his mother on her deathbed, when she asked me and H to always look out for each other, as we had only each other left.

But this wasn't true for me, at all. I had surrounded myself with a wonderful network of people. I had made an effort to do so and the same could not be said for H. What his mother had really meant when she said this was: 'my son has no one else, so I want you to look after him'. It was incredible how my sense of duty to others could even reach out to me from beyond the grave.

Through all this speculation, the pinnacle of it was the knowledge that, despite all that had happened (or failed to happen), I was a stubbornly independent woman and always had been. H had never taken care of me. I hadn't needed him to, but it would have been nice to know that should the occasion arise, he would step up to the plate. But, as you'd expect in a long-term relationship, occasions did arise—and every time, I had got myself through them alone.

In actuality, I may never have received this wake-up call if it were not for a chance encounter with another person, who would later become a very important person to me. This someone made me begin to question everything about the way I lived, piece by piece, starting with my existing relationship. It was what I needed—something big to happen, to show me how wrong my life was for me. Meeting this person and seeing a potential new life unfold before my eyes made me slowly begin to question everything about my relationship with H. Initially, I met this person with the intention of trying to help our relationship, but somewhere over the course of these meetings, this intention must have been skewed, instead giving me a glimpse of how my life could be if I dared to think the unthinkable: what if I were not with H?

If I had not dared to hope that the new relationship was a possible means of escape, I may have stayed longer to try and work it out with H, but our relationship had become a desert with no mirage of recovery on the horizon. Ours was not a partnership that could be brought back from the brink. It would have been a catastrophic mistake for me to stay in that relationship. He was not what I needed.

Appropriately enough, it was approaching the New Year when I decided to make a change. The first Christmas after I met that certain someone, I was miserable. We were out of contact due to family commitments and we missed each other to a frightening degree; at the time, we were only friends, officially speaking. Moreover, my relationship with H was on tenterhooks. It was uncertain and unstable. I felt strongly that I was on a precipice of change, and if I was to seek a potentially better life, I was struggling to see how, where and if H could fit into the equation. I was willing to take a huge risk. The following few days loomed dauntingly over me, not least because I knew they would be fraught with difficult decisions.

Every fibre of my being was screaming out to take a chance and chase the unknown. I could not get over an overwhelming feeling that I did not want to spend the rest of my life wondering what might have been. It was stronger than any other feeling; I had to take the plunge. It was a bigger decision I would have ever allowed myself to make previously, but I had to make this move, as there was no doubt that I had fallen in love with someone else.

When the New Year came around, I forced myself to make the decision to separate myself from those two major forces in my life. I had to be alone to clear my head and experience what it felt like to be completely uninhibited. Without outside influences, I could take stock of what it was I truly wanted. In order to be free of the stress, I hid myself away. I booked into a spa over a long weekend at the end of January—my birthday weekend, as it happened. I spent it completely alone. Somehow, it seemed fitting.

I discovered that I didn't really miss H—much as I did not want to acknowledge it at that time. I had been starved of my own company for so long that I was just starting to enjoy being me and nothing else. I had always felt a great sense of freedom in being alone and it was liberating. However, the person that I did miss was my new interest .... I tried to ignore these feelings but I should have been listening to them instead of trying to force them out, as they eventually overcame me regardless.

Within the ebb and flow of my agonising analysis, I switched back and forth between two states; the part of me that questioned how I could ever consider severing my loyalty to H after thirteen long years together, and the part that knew I could no longer live my life for other people.

I had a revelation: you cannot be responsible for others or their actions. Neither can you be responsible for their lack of action. You cannot live your life for others. You only get one life, you owe it to yourself to live every day to its fullest, and in order to do that, you must live primarily for yourself. Enjoy all the small things and look forward to the simple things. Have regrets about things you did, not things you never did. If you never ventured to explore something because there was a risk that you feared, you will only regret your lack of action later.

I realised, then, that I am a person who needs to have independence and have no one who is dependent on me; I need to be given space in order to be close to someone. If I had stayed, it would have been for all the wrong reasons and eventually, over time, my ill-chosen decisions would have begun to chip away at me and would ultimately have led to a failure later in the relationship. In short, staying for reasons of morals served no beneficial purpose to either H nor me. It would only have been my downfall. I was in danger of turning as transparent as cellophane, slowly on my way to becoming invisible.

At that moment in my life, I took the biggest leap of faith so far in all my short, unlived life. The conclusion was blindingly obvious: that thirteen years in that relationship paled in comparison with the rest of my life. I made a decision. I somehow found the strength to do what I knew I had to do.

I walked away.

There was unpleasantness, there was discomfort, and there was guilt—but there was necessity, too.

Revelations

You might now be wondering why I put up with all of that for so long. To be fair, H did try and warn me. He often said over the years: 'You could do better.' I said I chose to stay because I loved him. At the time, I had no comparable point of reference; he wasn't beating me, he wasn't a drunk, he didn't cheat on me with other women. So, I figured that it couldn't have been that bad.

Or else you might be wondering: 'If H was so bad, why did you stay for him for all that time?' A fair question. One thing is for sure; my perseverance with H was not simply in order to play the role of a martyr. I am strong and stoical and genuinely thought that our life together was fine. It is just that I had fallen into a rut, as we all can. I had been so young when we got together and he was simply the wrong companion for me—but I could not discover myself while handling the pressure of someone who needed so much from me.

It was not that H was selfish, exactly, but he was quite self-centred and spent his life all in one place. As a result of this, he had not the necessary experience to look out for himself, let alone me. In walking away I got to keep my independent streak, but I knew that it was he who was losing everything because he had built no support network around himself. So considering separating from him had me feeling like a heartless bitch. To some extent, I will always feel this way, but that does not change the fact that I had the opportunity to move on and had to take it.

H was my best friend and he relied on me so completely. In many ways, we felt like a good match—but 13 years passed without our acknowledging that things were going seriously wrong … It's a strange phenomenon. In lots of ways, I still loved H. It took me a while to realise that this love no longer encompassed romantic feelings and that without these, we didn't have a relationship.

For a significant proportion of the time we spent together, the difficulties I faced with H I attributed to 'going through a rough patch'. All we needed was to work a little harder at it. Circumstances had got in the way; two family deaths, for instance. It is amazing how many excuses one will make before acting.

After I realised what was going on, I still hesitated. We had been together so long and he promised to try harder at working to fix what was broken between us. I knew it was too late for this but I believe in second chances and knew that if I left, I would be abandoning him, as there was no one else in his life who he was close to.

But this is the thinking of a caregiver, not a partner. This role comes in many different forms but it is not necessary to employ this level of protectiveness over another adult with free will. It is not a passionate or romantic view, where both are choosing to be together because it will strengthen them in the relationship.

I think that as women, our instinct is to nurture and try to 'fix' things, but of course, not everything can be fixed. One of the biggest lessons I have learnt (and not just from my relationship with H) is that you cannot be responsible for another capable adult. Sometimes you have to just stand aside and let them make their own journey; which may include letting them make their own mistakes. As much as you love them, you may have to admit that you cannot help them. It's up to them. Ultimately, this may include walking away—as painful as this may be because you love them, at some point they must be left to make the journey they need to make on their own.

I was very preoccupied with making H comfortable—that is to say, comfortable to the highest level that he would allow himself to be, even with my encouragement. This only served to exacerbate the sensation of existing as a caregiver to him. All I succeeded in doing was creating an environment where I was walking on egg shells the whole time to avoid doing anything which could upset the delicate balance. I created a situation where he had become dependent on me, making it harder later to extract myself from the relationship.

Although not consciously recognising it at the time, the love I experienced in my past relationship with H was one where I came to fear that if I did not behave in certain ways and meet certain expectations, I would lose him. Much as I fully accept my responsibility for setting the bar at these expectations, at the time my fear stemmed from the fact that I had lost confidence and my sense of self. Being with him, whilst far from ideal, was a better prospect than being alone. My identity became that of a person who could make him happy. In this way, I allowed myself to be drawn into a conditional love relationship.

I failed to recognise the fundamental flaw in this; no matter what I did for him, he still did not love me in the way I needed to be loved and he could not love himself, no matter how much I loved him. I was too close to my own personal situation to see that H and I had separate journeys to make. Once I had some breathing space, I gained clarity of vision; it was impossible to see how, by travelling our life's journey's together, we could not both be successful in gaining what we each needed, because our goals were worlds apart.

There were so many things about him which were fundamentally different to me. Whereas I was good with people, he was not. I had better communication skills and relationship-building skills. I was adept at selling my attributes when needed. Since leaving University I had worked hard at every job I'd ever had, progressing and developing my career with every move I made, making friends along the way.

H did not like socialising. He made excuses as to why he did not want to come to social events. I'd repeatedly invite him and we would argue about it—I quickly realised that if I had to wait for him to come with me, I wouldn't go to any events I enjoyed, so I went alone. It brought me freedom and relieved him of any sense of duty.

Instead of questioning mine and H's level of incompatibility, I simply justified it all with the idea that 'opposites attract'. My awakening happened quite gradually—our differences built up to a point where they were no longer tolerable. One does not see things this way during the snapshots of time in which they are happening; during the relationship, I felt that I was doing everything to make him happy. Even towards what was inevitably the end of our relationship, I was very reluctant to give up on H. But he had given up on him—nothing I did would have made any difference. He didn't love himself enough, so he was unable to love me fully. He was empty of the emotions needed to keep our relationship reciprocal.

After I met someone new, I started to question things about my life and relationship. There was a shift within me, a point where I came to realise that I was more scared of how much I had lost myself than I was of losing H. I had been clinging on to the wrong thing, thinking I would be unhappier if I lost my partner than if I lost myself. Because I am fundamentally a self-sufficient person, I saw that my behaviour of staying in a relationship simply because I didn't want to face the alternative was not indicative of my independent streak.

I think it is common for people to stay in relationships for fear of the unknown. If they were to break up, they could not envision where their life would lead them. I know this just from observing and discussing relationships with family and several friends. We desperately cling on to a detrimental relationship, letting the years pass us by, having convinced ourselves that we would genuinely be worse off without that relationship.

I got into this situation because—probably just like others in undesirable relationships—I had become emotionally reliant on my partner; I am equally sure H was the same way. This ultimately meant that we crippled ourselves into not being able to walk away with ease.

After I had left H, my friends and family closed ranks (as often happens) making all the right sympathetic noises and comments:

'You did everything for him!'

'You were always there for him!'

'He had you at his beck and call!'

'He needed too much and took too much from you!'

Yes, all these things were true .... But at the same time, I don't place all the blame at H's feet. I played my role in all this when I allowed our relationship to deteriorate, simply by not saying anything or standing up for myself. I had poured so much of my efforts into satisfying his needs that I had ignored—worse, forgotten—about mine. I thought I was a strong, confident, successful woman but this was only the case outside of mine and H's relationship. Because of this, I realised I was not the well-rounded person I thought I was. I allowed and agreed and submitted to things which I could see were degrading and humiliating once I had awoken from my heavy sleep—his treatment of me whenever I tried to spend the night with him being the most prevalent example.

I think both H and I were complacent; I didn't think that sort of thing could happen to me and he was lulled into a false sense of security, believing that no matter how little effort he made and however he treated me I would always stay at his side. That last Christmas we spent together, we had a conversation about the future of our relationship—and more to the point, the possibility that we did not have a future. Even then, he did not try to apologise for what had been wrong all those years, or confess that he knew he had not pulled his weight and could try harder.

An environment of full on dependency was left to fester for all those years. Why would H challenge this safety blanket when I had voluntarily laid it down for him? While it is true that, if he loved me, he wouldn't have taken advantage in this way, the key point is that it takes two. It always takes two. In a stable adult-to-adult relationship, where you both care about each other's welfare and the fairness of sharing responsibilities, one would stand up and make an effort if he or she saw the other making all the effort. It's in the job description: 'partnership'.

As a result, I now no longer believe in loving someone 'no matter what'. Some situations are unacceptable and if you are sacrificing too much, you should not simply accept 'no matter what' just because you love that person.

You could view our situation through romantic eyes and claim it was lovely that I was his everything, that I was always on his mind and that he needed me. I hate the cliché: 'You complete me!' or the referral to someone's partner as their 'better half'. If anything, being with H left me feeling incomplete—besides which, even if I did believe in such a thing as a 'better half', he was certainly not my better half!

I do not buy into these romantic notions that this is what makes a solid relationship, or even a passionate whirlwind of romance. I am not unromantic but I do not believe that 'Hallmark/Hollywood' romance is sustainable, or realistic. I wanted to be with someone who was whole and didn't need me to complete them. My experience of being somebody else's 'completion' was that it was too much responsibility.

Life can deal some very difficult cards but we have the choice as to how we play them. We always have a choice and responsibility. No matter how dire the situation, there is always more than one option for how we deal with it; our lives are dependent on the decisions we make—or indeed, avoid making.

I realised that this was exactly what I had been doing; going along with the day-to-day, refusing to make any decisions. Then, the day-to-day became the month-to-month and the year-to-year. Frighteningly, I realised that my life had slipped past me without my noticing and this was no one's fault but my own. There was no point claiming that life had dealt me a bad hand; I had to take responsibility for the fact that I was in my 30s and had not lived. I had been with H since I was 18, so my 20s had passed me by, empty of the rich experiences and usual landmarks of growing up—all because I had stayed with a man who did not want to develop in any area of his life. Much as I had moved forward significantly more than H, I was stunted in my natural progression simply because I had not taken the ample opportunity to stop and question what the hell I was doing!

'What were you doing all that time?' I was asked when I recounted this story to SJ, a good friend of mine. I hesitated.

'I lost my 20s,' I finally replied. I then realised the power of this statement and the sadness of its truthfulness, though I felt it in a detached way, as though I was talking of someone else's life. Then the gravity of it hit me.

'I lost my 20s!' I repeated in surprise rather than indignity. I had spent nearly 13 years going to every social event by myself. I had never gone to any family events with my partner; over the years I attended every friends' and family members' wedding on my own.

'Didn't your family say to you "wake up"!?' asked SJ incredulously, when she heard of this.

'Wake up.' … It is a phrase which has come to me so many times. It strikes me because coming away from my relationship with H was exactly like waking up; I lost my 20s because I sleep-walked through them. I ran to H's side all those years, trying to make him happy and keep up the pace before I found myself out of breath. It was killing the real me.

'When you say you lost your 20s … ' continued SJ, 'Isn't that what we do? You give your whole heart to someone and in doing so, lose yourself. You try your best but they still walk away and you are left asking: "What's wrong with me?" And the only answer is that you were stupid enough to let them walk away with a part of you. In break-ups, we fight over possessions and property, mutual friends and child access but we don't say "Oh, and give me back the part of me you stole."' (SJ will be the source of many more eloquent and memorable quotes to come!)

It rings true and backs up all I have said about keeping yourself over your partner. It is fortunate that my eventful 30s have more than made up for my 20s!

What a Difference
a T Makes

T here was one aspect of H's personality that was so important to him that it smothered any chance he had of being a well-rounded, balanced person. It was the single thing upon which he blamed all his other failings. He blamed it for his previous relationship problems. He blamed it for his lack of a successful career, despite his excellent education. In short, he allowed this one aspect of his personality to cripple him.

He was a transvestite.

I know that for many women, this can come as quite a shock. I know that for some women they come to this knowledge believing they have been happily married for many years and are comfortable in the belief that they know everything there is to know about each other, until one day her husband sits her down and explains that there is a side to his personality which he has never shared with her. It is a huge part of his identity that he denied for his whole life. He explains that he can no longer continue to do so, as he feels he is living a lie; he confesses that he is a transvestite. He says he enjoys dressing in women's clothes. He wishes to start expressing his feminine side. This can be devastating.

If you were in that situation, it is quite possible that, even if you were not overly concerned about his cross-dressing, it would probably blow your world apart. The life you have built together would feel like a lie. You might start to question who your husband really is and wonder if you even know the man you married; if he could keep such a huge secret, he may be lying about all other aspects of your life together.

I was not put in a dissimilar situation, in that I did not know at the very beginning of our relationship H was a transvestite—however, the scenario above was not particularly the case with H and me. I was 19 at the time and didn't fully understand what transvestism entailed or what I was getting into. We had been dating for nearly a year and he said he had something to confess about himself which he had not told me about. Naturally, I was worried and he took his time skirting around the subject. It was then that I saw the anguish that afflicts people who must make this kind of confession; it was so impossibly distressing for H to say the words that in the end he had to write it on a piece of paper and show me.

That memory is as clear to me as if I had unfolded that piece of paper and read its monumental contents just yesterday. I didn't think about any issues of betrayal, nor was I angry that he had kept this from me. His discomfort and emotional pain was so obvious that I just wanted to comfort him. I had fallen in love with him. I didn't really know what being a transvestite was or what it meant and its implications on our relationship.

'I don't understand it but I love you and am willing to support you, however you need me to,' was my response. I gave my full support—an empty and fruitless exercise, as I could not embrace his identity for him whatever I tried. Equally, H would have forgiven me if I had said that his transvestism was not something I wanted any part of and that the relationship should be brought to an end. He may even have expected me to say something of the sort.

Despite my acceptance in H eyes, his transvestism overshadowed his entire personality; in reality, what really hindered him was his lack of self-acceptance. He was in the closet. His whole life, his whole outward image, was a lie.

I think the problems in my and H's relationship stemmed not from him being a transvestite, but from his inability to accept his identity as such. Our relationship breakdown is an example of how trans issues can be a destructive force in a relationship; women who have trans partners can find the dynamics of the relationship changing so that every little thing becomes about how (s)he is transgendered. It can take over—though every relationship has something unique to it that is a cause of stress on each partner. Usually there are many factors; the breakup of a relationship is never about just one thing. The issue is how couples face problems and work together to resolve them.

Being trans is part of who someone is, not the whole. You can make it into a problem even if it is not; anything you view as a 'problem' becomes a problem if you label it as such. If you view it simply as an issue you have to deal with as best you can, you can move on. The alternative is that it becomes all-consuming and all-encompassing—you can blame everything that is failing in your life on it.

Particularly in partnerships, problems are as big as you make them. Feeding off each other, I think H and I jointly made his transvestism a huge issue in the end. It was probably the biggest single problem in our relationship. I say this because, while there were other issues that needed working on, they all seemed to relate back to his transvestism.

We were not brave enough to tackle it early or to fix it constructively. Please understand that when I say 'fix' it, I do not mean curing H of being a transvestite—I mean dealing with issues when they arose early in the relationship, you could argue I wasted years. Two things could have happened if I had been more willing to rock the boat in the early days; we could have faced things head on and continued to do so throughout our relationship, becoming stronger for it (and who knows where we would be) or I may have sooner come to the conclusion that I could not help H.

Whereas someone who drinks too heavily can seek support from Alcoholics Anonymous, there is very little backing for trans people and their partners. Passing over the fact that, contrary to alcoholism, being transgender is a part of identity rather than a thing to be curbed and controlled, even professionals in the field of transgender do not fully understand all the intricacies of how these issues can affect a relationship.

Let's assume that, in any relationship, there will come a time when the going gets tough and there is something that the two individuals need to work on together in order to move on. Unless they have been successful in working it out, there may come a point when they have tried everything imaginable and given it their best, to no avail. In that situation, you may question your loyalty to the relationship and decide enough is enough. You have exhausted all options—and yourself—in the process. In this case, the very worst thing you can do is give up on yourself, as I did. But when you have invested all your efforts in something, it is hard to see the line you have crossed in the process.

I remained one hundred per cent supportive of H's transvestism from the day he came out to me until the very end of our relationship. I was willing to do anything I could, in any way, to encourage him to be himself and be comfortable with the fact that this was a side of his personality which was not going to go away—no matter how many times he binged and purged, buying tons of women's clothes and throwing them all away again.

One might think that my acceptance would ease his mind a little, but he simply could not live with his transvestism in any comfortable way. He did seek some comfort in the various online communities for trans people. It may have helped him a little, but it also transpired to be the beginning of our downfall as a couple; it opened the door for me to find love elsewhere.

The person I met was someone I came into contact with during an earnest attempt to support my existing partner. H built a profile for me on a trans community website and added a photograph. This caused me no concern at the time and he reasoned that, if I could chat to people online as a partner of someone who was a transvestite, then I might be able to get others' advice to help him.

During the course of this correspondence, someone caught mine and H's attention: Nicci. We discussed the possibility of both of us going to meet her in person. Eventually, we agreed that I should go—alone. H figured he didn't really need to be there, as I would probably do all the talking anyway and could let him know how it went later. I was the one who was good with people, after all.

I returned home and dutifully reported back on the meeting. H asked if I thought that this person could help us and I said that I certainly thought so. I will never know for sure, but I suspect that my subconscious knew the truth behind these words; it was me I felt she could help, not me and H as a couple. If anyone had suggested this at the time, I would have strongly denied thinking any such thing. I continued to meet Nicci. Our meetings will stick with me for a long time to come. We connected right away and I was so honest with her. I even told her that H and I had not had a physical relationship for years—she asked me if I was bothered about not having sex. I replied that I didn't mind; it was about being with the right person and if you love one another, then sex is not so important. I recall expressing passionately that I loved H and I could never, ever, foresee not being with him. I said that I would never do anything to jeopardise our relationship.

I added that people overrate sex and that after you have been together for 13 years, it was normal for the sex to die out—wasn't it? I could never have dreamt that this was the beginning of the end of my long-term relationship. Even as I said these words I don't think I truly believed them; because they were H's words and not mine.

An Ideal
Relationship?

People often find love when they are not looking for it. It comes at you out of the blue and can be very inconvenient! It doesn't always happen at the 'right' time. It could simply be that it was exactly what both parties needed at the time—only we cannot see it because we purposefully put barriers in the way. Many of us may have a plan for life and are reluctant to do anything that may block that path for which we have planned. I do not believe that it is a coincidence or fate that you meet people during times of transition. If you are happy with yourself, others will also see something in you that they find attractive. That is no accident.

In my and Nicci's case we were both very clear that we would not be unfaithful to our then partners by starting a relationship together at that point. We would not act until we had decided on the right course for each of us in regards to our existing relationships. During this time we agreed to put our friendship on hold and deal with our individual situations.

I did not choose Nicci over H. I couldn't even consider it. Quite apart from anything else, in the time apart from one another, I had no idea what Nicci was thinking; I considered the possibility that she had decided she and I were never meant to be, instead choosing to try and work things out with her ex-partner (from whom she had been separated for some time). Not knowing anything about Nicci's thoughts was exactly the situation I wanted. I wanted to make my decision based solely on whether or not it was the right thing for me to remain in a relationship with H.

It wasn't. I wanted a partner who could be themselves because I strongly believed that only in fully being yourself can you properly give to the other person. I realised that the one person to whom I had dedicated my life was by far the biggest drain on me; the negativity and stunted emotional growth came from not realising sooner that the welfare of another adult was simply not my responsibility. H's need for me was too great and it was suffocating.

I began to wonder what I could achieve with someone by my side who was actively encouraging me, just by being themselves and being a real, whole person with ambitions for themselves—ambitions that they actually went after, rather than permanently dreaming. I wanted to live every day to its fullest. I wanted to be loved in the way I needed.

I had met someone who had given me a glimpse of how things could be different and better. Thoughts of the possibilities of this started to grow and flourish within me; Nicci had shown a genuine interest in me as a person and as such, she had planted the seed of an idea in my mind—the idea that there was something about me that was worth loving. Moreover, it was in a different way to how I had experienced being loved up to that point. I was having visions of how a relationship could be if you both worked at enriching each other, encouraged one another to have goals outside of the relationship and worked together towards achieving those goals. This was what a good relationship looked like; the ability to have one's own independent interests, and bring these back to the relationship, providing more to share with one another.

Though what I felt was obvious to me, I didn't know whether my feelings were strong enough to change my whole life and turn everything upside down. Those decisions seemed like impossible ones at the time, but I soon realised that the reality of staying with H would mean severing all ties with Nicci, which was inconceivable.

'You can forget about Nicci. We can put it behind us,' pleaded H at the end. 'But you are just not trying.'

It took a lot of strength to reply with the painful truth that the issue was that I did not want to forget Nicci.

I couldn't bring myself to forget her. We had clicked. In one of our various discussions about relationships in general, we discussed what seemed like a perfect formula for a relationship. On hearing it described, it made so much sense; there was clarity and purpose. It was a recipe with ingredients that might just work. Her description was of a partnership in which you both have your own lives and dreams; things you want to experience that you can share. Only then can you achieve—with the other person encouraging you every step of the way. As a consequence, you will both develop and grow. We had this conversation during a weak moment of our temporary period of supposed incommunicado. The conversation gave me hope and it made me want to be with her so deeply, even though I didn't know if this was even possible at that time.

In the end, that which had seemed impossible became necessary. I found I could actually end a thirteen year relationship to pursue a life which I thought would be better, and additionally no longer felt that this was purely selfish. How could I pass up the opportunity to live a full life? When I first started to have feelings for Nicci, I reasoned it was not meant to be; that we had met at the wrong time in life and so on and so forth.

We even said to one another: 'Where were you years ago?' The implication being that Nicci and I were both tied to other people and that was that—I nearly dismissed the idea of a relationship with her because of it.

'It wasn't meant to be,' was something else we said.

It's fortunate that I believe in making your own destiny, because this meant that it wasn't the end of the story. I do believe that fate plays a part, but equally I believe that everybody has a choice in any given situation—however hard that choice may be to make. Over the course of getting to know Nicci, I realised that it was a golden opportunity I had to take and that, prior to that point, I just hadn't understood the significance of Nicci coming into my life. I could have stubbornly ignored my growing feelings that I was in the wrong relationship—but that would have led me nowhere. At some point the question of 'How could I?' became a question of 'How can I not?'

Our friendship started tentatively. Nicci and I chatted freely via email and got on well, building our bond until, naturally, we suggested meeting up. I met her in a smart hotel lobby in central London. I was nervous; anxious from the many warnings about meeting up with people who you only know from the Internet. Yet, something about that meeting made me want to look my best; to dress up—and yes, even to look attractive.

The most memorable thing that struck me was how open Nicci was. It is the first thing that springs to mind when people ask what it was that first attracted me to her. She had an 'I don't care what people think of me' attitude, a sort of 'I am who I am and if you don't accept me, so be it,' air. I found this very refreshing. She was willing to be herself, unguarded, not worried if people did not like her for who she was. She would not present herself as a different person in public for other people's benefit. Neither was she restricted by the kinds of neurotic nuances that afflict many of us. She had come closer to living her life the way that is best for her than anyone I had ever met.

There was no game playing with Nicci, no cloak and dagger; what you saw was what you got. Nicci's biggest fight for her beliefs and values was a sign that she was being constantly, unselfconsciously true to herself. To this day, the one thing that she is not willing to sacrifice or compromise on for anyone—me included—is pretending to be someone she is not. She pretended to be someone she wasn't for years before she was 'out' about being transgender. She has been there, done that, got the T-shirt (so to speak) and will never go back to how she was before. She is defiant about it—and rightly so. Not only that, but she believes in it for everyone, not just herself. In this way, she lives a genuinely pure, free life.

I was very surprised, during that first meeting, by how easy she was to talk to. I usually find it easy enough to start up casual conversations, but we talked about the most intimate topics imaginable, including the relationship problems between H and me. Of course, this is what we had met up to discuss but she was virtually a stranger and I opened up to her completely, giving her all whole sorry story about my and H's sexual relationship (or lack thereof).

I clearly remember one point in the conversation when Nicci leaned over to me and placed her hand on my leg. I did not think too much of it, as it was all very natural and seemingly innocent in the context of our conversation—beside which, she seemed to be a naturally tactile person. Nonetheless, I felt something in that touch. I can't think of any other words to describe the sensation that have not been overused many times before, but I will say that I felt a spark, like an electric shock.

I didn't know at that first meeting how exactly Nicci fitted into my life and future decisions, but deep down, I felt that somehow, she had a huge part to play. With Nicci, I could see the opportunity not only to free myself, but to encourage an exploration of the real me, with whom I had lost contact during the long relationship with H. No longer would I shrink away from life in order to make someone else happy.

After our first meeting, we were both on the Internet at the first opportunity to say how much we both enjoyed our meeting. Nicci confessed to having shared things with me she had never shared with anyone else. She had also found me very easy to talk to.

The question of sex came up more than once. I had no idea how huge a question that was to become. Not only did I discover that I have a healthy appetite for physical affection with a partner, but Nicci discovered the same thing during the course of our conversations. These days, the level of sex I enjoy is reflective of my and Nicci's overall relationship. It was the first real indication I had of how much sex matters. Essentially, Nicci and I are very sexually compatible and have both experienced relationships where physical affection was low on our partners' agenda. This was immediately apparent to Nicci and me the first time we kissed; as corny as it sounds, the only description I have is that I had a sensation like I was almost literally melting in Nicci's arms.

'That felt like you had never been kissed before,' were her first words to me afterwards.

The truth was, I hadn't. I had certainly never in my life been kissed like *that* before. There was an undeniably strong connection between us and it was a light bulb moment of realisation about what I had been missing. I wanted more of it. I had been denying that a physical relationship was important to me and it wasn't enough just to love the person and enjoy spending time in their company; I realised perhaps the obvious—that such as relationship is essentially a friendship, not typical of a lover or partner.

Before that kiss, Nicci and I had been just friends and only friends. Although I had feelings which I had been denying, my sense of duty, honour, 'right and wrong' kicked in immediately and I told H what had happened at the first opportunity. His reaction pinpoints the beginning of the landslide that was the ending of our relationship; he was not bothered that I had kissed someone else.

'I don't give you the physical side of the relationship you want, so you might as well get it from someone else,' was his response.

I reeled at this shocking statement. I asked him how he felt, in disbelief. He responded that he couldn't feel anything. My world started to spin out of all recognition; it wasn't that he 'couldn't', it was that he couldn't be bothered. He didn't have the desire. H's disinterest in my confession was degrading and humiliating to me, but he did not recognise this.

The kiss had taken place just before that first Christmas. Nicci and I were out of touch but over the holiday period, H confessed that he had come to find the act of kissing to be disgusting. Those were his actual words, which I will never forget; it was his complacency that I found so degrading. H did not want to split up. He said he was worried about our future. Although he had dropped this bombshell, he still wanted us to be together, expecting me to want to continue in a relationship with someone who had only just told me he didn't like kissing. And he continued to do absolutely nothing, make no effort whatsoever, to salvage what we had. He never thought I would actually leave him— unbelievably, at this point I still thought I wouldn't either. I don't think either of us could see it was already over.

After we took a break over New Year, we made an attempt to rekindle the relationship over a romantic Valentine's weekend. H suggested it but it was a bitter gesture, as one of his 'principles' over the years we had been together was that he didn't 'believe' in Valentine's Day. We tried for the very first time in years (yes, literally years) to have sex. Inevitably, it wasn't very successful.

Perversely, I felt terrible guilt .... Guilt that I was cheating on Nicci! I felt this despite the fact that Nicci and I had not consummated our feelings any more than one kiss; my morals did not allow me to go any further, much as I desperately wanted to. By lying back and not mentally participating in sex with H, I felt dirty and ashamed that the beautiful and luxurious hotel bedroom was wasted that Valentine's Day. I realise now that the real reason I felt dirty was because the person I was really cheating on was me—I was betraying how I really felt. To top it all off, although Nicci and I had not been in contact, she weakened and sent me a Valentine's text. I was over the moon with forbidden excitement. It was also the first time in my relationship with H I had hidden something from my partner and I knew I shouldn't have.

Inevitably trying to rekindle the relationship with H was not working. During my time in voluntary isolation from Nicci, I contacted her briefly only to tell her that I needed more time to think without contact. We both confessed, to my absolute delight, that what we wanted was to have a relationship. I took more alone time, just to see how it felt—it felt great. I have always been very comfortable alone; I would even go so far as to say that I love my own company. That, I realised, was fundamental to my being—the fully rounded me that I am meant to be. In spending my life trying to cater for someone else's happiness, I had given myself no opportunity over all those years to enjoy my own company. This part of the relationship was largely what had strangled and suffocated me.

Continuing on my journey of overturning everything in my life, I chose a complete career change and was thrilled to be offered a job in that field. I promptly accepted. In addition, I went on holiday abroad with a friend. Neither of these things had anything to do with romantic relationships and I knew—that should I choose—I could live a good life and be happy by myself. I didn't need to be in a relationship to feel whole.

It may have been that I only needed me, but I couldn't wait any longer for my wants. Nicci and I had been in contact but had not seen each other for a while and were missing each other very much. There was no doubt at this point that we were in love and didn't want to stay apart for another minute. The rest, as they say, is history—though of course, the story does not end. My relationship with Nicci brought its own story and a new outlook.

In the spirit of living every day as if it is your last, the life I lived just in that first year from splitting with H and starting a relationship with Nicci was, to me, phenomenal. Just some of the experiences I had were: standing up in front of 200 people and delivering a day's training session alongside my partner with fantastic praise from delegates; dancing with her at a 65th birthday party I organised for my mum; dancing in a full length ball gown at the Rivoli ballroom and watching my partner perform ballet in a studio; I took singing lessons; attended a Stonewall conference in the houses of parliament; met the founders of a charity and continue to work with them; went to a Rugby match and loved it as I never would have expected; attended the best New Year's party ever; and went to a music gig completely on my own and loved the freedom that it brought.

One of the biggest events for me was buying my own gorgeous

property in an area lovelier than I had ever before dreamed possible, what with the finance and the management of it. I had a house-warming party and have hosted several dinner parties. I got to have Christmas dinner in my own home with my family and partner around me. In my new home with my new life, I started researching and writing a book.

With each month that passed, I looked back and couldn't believe what I had been missing and how much I was experiencing. Some of it may seem mundane and ordinary to others but to me it was a constant adventure that proved, time and time again, that I had made the right decision. For the first time ever, I was living life to the full.

I believe that life's path throws stones in our way for a reason and we shouldn't necessarily dismiss them; after all, plans change, dreams change, and people change.

Rules of Attraction

Nicci and I were starting a fresh relationship together and agreed to discuss and lay down the rules we felt necessary in order to self-preserve. We discussed all our thoughts, past experiences and what we were willing, or not, to accept. Each of us was determined not to make the same mistakes as in the last relationship. As highly unromantic as that sounds, I assure you we released our animal instincts first (but let's save that for later).

Although not necessarily romantic, the conversations we had about what type of relationship we both wanted were highly satisfying. They were deep and intense and very loving. We agreed that our only expectation of the other person was for them not to purposefully hurt us. The manner of body language Nicci communicated towards me when discussing this was very tender. She expressed promises of always being open and honest at all times, no matter what. It seemed too good to be true and although not always easy to date, we continue to stick to what we agreed.

The basic premise is that, against convention, you do not have any expectations of the other person. Bin all the conventional, societal rules, roles and conventions you are supposed to follow in a relationship. Simple. You express unconditional love and support. You take care of your own needs and concentrate on what you want. Presuming you are both fairly reasonable, intelligent people and that you both love and care about one another, you will naturally fulfil each other's needs.

This may take a change, depending on your life experiences,

personality, etc. I believe there is a great deal of truth in the adage that if you love yourself, then others can love you. If you love yourself, then you take care of you and your needs. You are two adults in the relationship, therefore it should be a given that the other person can take care of themselves, and so you are not expelling all your energy in taking care of one another. This liberates you to concentrate on the actual relationship, showing each other affection and tenderness.

Most importantly of all, you do not complete each other. You are not two halves of a whole, but two whole beings, sharing your lives with each other. I can almost guarantee that if you both support this model, fully, there is success in it.

The two of you can share your unique experiences and thoughts on events and issues. You should both encourage talking about each other's feelings and desires in a friendly, uninterrupted context; each of you listening with genuine interest to continually grow your understanding of the other person. Nicci, for example, was very encouraging of me writing this book. She shared her thoughts and opinions on it and respected that, much as I loved some of them, I may not listen to all of them. She came on the journey with me as I shared each stage with her.

Equally, Nicci (about 18 months into our relationship) started to think about developing her own business. It was a risk but I supported and encouraged her to go after her dream, just as she had done for me. She asked for my opinion and valued it. I told others about what she does and helped generate contacts.

It is important to have different interests and things that you do on your own. This does not mean that you are living separate lives, of course there will be interests you share but it means that you are both living fuller lives and sharing these together. I have experienced this as being a very healthy model for a relationship.

If you have read John Gray's *Men Are From Mars, Women Are From Venus*, you will appreciate that men have a propensity towards freedom and independence. We might assume that in a large number of cases, men don't like to be nagged and—again, I am making a sweeping generalisation—that many women do like to know what their partners are up to where and when (quizzing them to that affect). This is a potential recipe for arguments; it will build resentment and tension, as the two want opposite things in the relationship. For it to work, fundamentally there has to be trust. If you start with trust as your foundation, the difference is resolvable.

In the above scenario, the same woman—let's call her Jane—may feel less of a need to fish for information about the movements of her partner if she truly trusts him. In return, the man is more likely to volunteer this information. Neither of you is asking permission of the other, it is about courtesy and respect, particularly if you live together. If you are both working from the basis that it is good for you to do different things apart, it is less likely for either of you to have an issue with the other enjoying a drink out with friends. There are no expectations; however, this must be an agreed version of the relationship from the beginning.

A startling realisation I had when I ended the relationship with H was that in the beginning, he always said I was a good influence on him. We all like to be flattered and adored and told that we are special and can make a difference. At first, he was proud that I was more outgoing than he was, and achieved more. This, although hidden under the surface, set up expectations that I was some sort of saviour for him.

As I have mentioned, only he could have made progress in his own life. At some point into our relationship the voracity with which I approached my career and social life became a source of resentment for him, although I didn't know this. He was envious I could pursue my own interests and he could not (or would not). When we were ending our relationship, H revealed that on the rare occasions we had socialised together, he felt I lit up the room. He felt confined to a darkened corner, while I circulated the room, lighting up faces, making people laugh as I flowed around the party. He said he couldn't stand it, and that it was one of the reasons why he stopped socialising with me. I never had any idea that this is how he felt and it sickened me that he could somehow twist his lack of social skills into something that was my fault. Also it seemed rather an extreme view to have of me and I wondered if he had built it up as something more than it was by not talking about it.

After learning this, close friends have all commented that he should have been proud to have a partner who was so naturally adept at being a fun-loving people-person, putting others at ease. As I have said, to develop, the progress has to come from within you—and both you and your partner have to follow your paths religiously for them to work out the way they should. It isn't always easy, but anything really worthwhile should also be a challenge to be worked at. The reward and the pay-off is as high as they come; a better life. And I mean real living—I now enjoy every day for all the little things, simply because I am utterly and blissfully free to be exactly the person I am, and be loved for it unconditionally, with no pressure of expectation from my partner. If I have an ability 'to light up a room' it would now be cherished by my partner.

It is amazing what you can achieve when someone else believes in you. When someone invests an interest in your hopes and ambitions, you conquer them all with that person by your side. Your self-confidence and self-belief is bolstered and anything becomes possible. You become more secure in your own self-worth. Fundamentally, you are doing it for you, but if you can share it and celebrate it together it becomes a bonus and there is an added incentive.

I have only ever encouraged Nicci to stay true to herself. Some days I have chastised her—kindly—when her confidence has flagged. Yes, the 'fuck you all, I am who I am' attitude she had when I met her was what attracted me in first place and its continuation was never dependent on my presence in Nicci's life, but nonetheless we all have moments of weakness and self-doubt. During these times, I have been there to remind her of who she is, not to tell her who to be. I gently remind her of all that she has gone through to get where she is—the bravery she had shown in just being honest with the world. I could not (and would not) ever tell her who she has to be, or what she can or cannot do.

I maintain that, if friends and family visit, they accept her as she is. I would never insist that she does anything to make my family any more comfortable with her presence as my partner. It would be unfair and disrespectful. In essence, I accepted her to be herself in the spirit of the baseline in our relationship that we set and agreed upon.

Nicci and I have found that there is just one secret to maintaining openness and honesty in our relationship in a continually loving, sharing and non-argumentative manner. Like the golden rules of buying a property, it is so important it is worth repeating three times: 'no censorship, no censorship, no censorship'. This concept works two-fold. Not only does it apply to communication with the other person but also to looking inwards at your own behaviour.

It comes into play when you have something on your mind about which you must be honest to your partner; perhaps you don't feel they have been supporting you as much as you would like on an issue causing you discomfort, or else you are not happy about how they have behaved, something they said when you were out with friends. Rather than give a personal example, I invite you to imagine for yourself approaching your partner and saying: 'I need to have a no censorship conversation with you ....' Or alternatively, stating: 'No censorship: I am not happy about this ....'

Obviously, you will both be familiar with the concept by this point; most importantly, it gives the other person the opportunity to brace themselves for something they may be uncomfortable hearing— perhaps even something they would really rather not hear at all.

I believe that this works for Nicci and me. I have noticed that others feel that we communicate well.

'You are both willing to accept change and work with what you've got,' SJ observed. 'You are both so open-minded in the way you think about things as they come up, and discuss them. Because there is constant communication between the two of you, it does not build up—so you don't have arguments about stupid little things that got out of hand.'

I believe that Nicci and I don't argue about the little things because we are both generally laid back and the little things do not bother us. I believe people often do not discuss all the things they really should for fear of upsetting the other—I know I didn't with H. There are several things wrong with this. One is that you are censoring yourself if there is something bothering you. Two is that it is healthier to get things off your chest, and three is that you are not giving the other person the opportunity to share your problems with you, to let them prove that they can be supportive and sympathetic to your feelings. Lastly, discussing what bothers you is fundamental to being a fully well-rounded and adjusted adult who can satisfy your own needs.

Children have temper tantrums and they do not have the capacity to understand how this affects their relationships. As adults, we can see that when one behaves unreasonably towards someone else, they are very likely to mirror your behaviour and communicate in just as much of an unacceptable way. Instead of letting things that are bothering you go unsaid—which is unhealthy and unfair to both of you (I should know—I did it for thirteen years) you should open yourself up even over little things. I believe it is a key element of self-respect.

Crucially, all issues must be dealt with in the present. If you wait too long your partner could rightly ask: 'Why didn't you say anything at the time?' or 'Why are you bringing that up now?' If it is left to fester and raised it in the heat of the moment at a later date, it will cause all manner of discontent. Instead, it needs to be out in the open, acknowledged and discussed. Yes, it may have been something hurtful; we cannot change what has been done. Nevertheless, it must be forgiven, forgotten and left in the past. This is why it is important to make sure that you are satisfied with the outcome of the discussion before you try to move on.

I acknowledge that being this open is easier when you have had to learnt to accept yourself. It makes a difference when you have been on a journey such as Nicci's—or that of any transgendered person. Nicci has fought a difficult fight to come to terms with identity, shared this with others and decided to stand out in the world in order to find comfort. After that mountain, facing up to smaller issues and having honest conversations is probably a breeze compared to how many of us may feel about doing it—myself included. I absolutely hate confrontation but recognise at this point in my life that facing things is better in the long run than sticking your head in the sand.

Much as freedom from censorship is a great concept in any relationship, whether it be partners, friends or family, before you can rid your relationship of censorship, you must first deal with censorship within yourself. There is something particularly raw and exposing about executing non-censorship with your partner, and I think it is more successful when you have a truly deep understanding of who they are as a person and in return, they understand the real you. This is where the fear ramps up—exposing the real you and inviting a partner to expose the real them, involves risk. There is always a chance they might not accept you for who you are if you reveal certain aspects of yourself to them; they may feel you are not the person they once thought. That, in turn, makes you panic. 'What if they reject me?' you might ask yourself. The knowledge that the alternative is pointless will help you get past this; if you try too hard to be what you think they want, you will eventually and inevitably be discovered—even if that point comes when you are firmly trapped in an unhealthy relationship.

Self-revelation is not easy for all of us. Some people grow up in situations where they could not fully express their true thoughts and feelings—were not given the freedom to discover themselves openly, because it would have caused discomfort for their parents. However, it is vital to have the freedom to be your true self in any relationship. If either of you has not experienced this in childhood or adolescence, your partner's offer of an opportunity to be without restriction is likely to lead to a relationship that is stronger and will grow deeper. There is the risk that the other person may not accept you, but if they reject you, it will be clear that they are not the right person for you.

First and foremost, it is important to be yourself. Relationships must come second, as I truly believe someone else can only really love you when you love yourself. However, there is greater joy when they do accept you; you will know, for a fact, that they love you for exactly who you are, not a weak concept that you have built for them; some half person that is convenient for them to love.

In my and Nicci's relationship, it will not be my acceptance about the more unusual aspect of our relationship that I think will be the key to the sustainability of it. More likely, it will be that we enable and support each other to be ourselves with the use of encouragement. Nicci says to me that I am extraordinary (in the true definition of the term) in my attitude and outlook, and that should we ever split up, she would never find another woman with whom she could strike up quite the same relationship. Nonetheless, her strength of self is such that she knows that, if it came to it, she would rather be on her own and be true to herself than be in a relationship with someone who placed restrictions on her or was controlling in any way.

Not all of us have the level of bravery it takes to go it alone, or the bravado to say 'Hey, so if I end up without a partner, that's OK.' I think we have had a revelation, Nicci and I; we know that, if a relationship we had been in was so destroying to us, we potentially would be more likely to go it alone than stay in a relationship that is not working. For instance, I have a fabulous friend in her 50s, who is currently the happiest she has ever been in her life. She is on her own, yet she looks healthier and more fantastic than she ever did when she was in her relationship that wasn't working and which had led to a breakup. Then again, 'on her own' is not necessarily true; though she is single, this certainly does not mean that she is alone. The relationship you have with yourself and others close around you, like family, can be equally (if not more) satisfying.

The L Word

By now you may be curious about the relationship I am in; no: my partner is not gay and I am not a lesbian. As you may have surmised from the fact that I first met her on a website for trans people, Nicci is transgendered male-to-female. This is different from transvestism and being transsexual, in ways I will elaborate on later. In short, Nicci is physically male but identifies as female.

It would be wise to tackle one of the biggest misconceptions early on; that transgendered people are not necessary gay. Shocker! I apologise for the sarcasm but it really is a staggeringly huge mistake I have seen made too many times before. Being thought of as a lesbian is a common experience for women in a relationship with a trans partner—I am not offended if people make this assumption about me but on the other hand, given the choice I would rather they didn't, I suppose. I have no problem with lesbians (hence why I am not offended) but it is not what I identify as.

Why, then, does being transgendered not necessarily mean that you are gay? Because sex and gender are not the same thing. In short, your sex is between your legs and gender is between your ears—it is who you believe you are. You can feel your gender; most people know in their own mind if they are a woman or a man, without having to look south to confirm it.

However, here is where it gets complicated: Nicci is a woman and I am a woman and we are in love, but do not consider ourselves to be gay or lesbian—a fact that has caused some confusion for our various acquaintances!

'How can you want to be female ... and have a female partner ... and not be gay?' one of our friends asked of Nicci, with a confused expression on her face. She reports that her husband was also surprised to discover that Nicci was not interested in men.

She explained that, in her understanding, if a man dresses as a woman, he must be interested in men. It is my belief that she only became sure that this wasn't necessarily the case once Nicci started dating me and we had been together for a while. After all, it was not as though she could deny the fact! To this day, she struggles to get her head around it. Her thinking is mirrored by others we have met.

'You're not a lesbian, are you?' my own mother asked me in anticipated shock when first I told her about Nicci. It was her way of trying to understand the whole concept of her daughter in such unusual circumstances.

If there were no labels, people might rather ask what we are we into sexually, as opposed to our sexual orientation. A woman might say: 'I am turned on by having sex with men,' and a man might say: 'I am turned on by being tied up and whipped by either sex'. Another woman might say: 'I am turned on by having sex with a woman,' and a transvestite man might say: 'I am turned on by dressing up in women's clothing.' But I understand labelling and participate as much as everyone else, because to some extent we must. People have unwittingly answered the question of my sexual orientation by way of genuine confusion: 'I don't know how I can classify you.'

One of my tasks while writing this book was to interview some of the people who are close to Nicci and me in order to understand their expectations and assumptions. 'I don't think that you are straight,' said SJ, as a friend and interviewee. 'I use "straight" in the traditional sense, but then, there is nothing traditional about your relationship. It's just that there is nothing about anything I see in your relationship which is traditional—yet everything I have seen has been very positive.'

'For those who misunderstand transgender, it's hard to box Nicci as being gay because she is with you, a woman,' they added.

When considering gay relationships—two biological men, or two biological women—some outsiders still like to try and restore some kind of natural order to things. They will ask who is the 'man' and who is the 'woman' in the relationship and who 'wears the trousers'. I think this is a way of asking who is the more dominant in the bedroom; who is the 'top', who is the 'bottom'. I am sure this is not a question that is at the forefront of people's minds when they first encounter a heterosexual couple, so why it should be any more so for a gay couple or a trans couple is beyond me.

Yet I understand that it is confusing. I asked other women who are in a relationship with a transgendered woman how they defined their sexuality.

'I have always classified myself as bi-curious with a preference for men,' one said. 'I have never had any kind of relationship with another genetic female; but I do find some transgendered male-to-females sexually attractive. Usually, the closer they are to 'pre-op', the more attractive I find them … I don't go for the 'guy-in-a-dress' look.

'I did struggle with this for a while at the beginning of dating my first trans partner; although I never thought of myself as bi-curious, actually finding myself dating a man who sometimes dressed as a girl and finding the female part attractive was initially very confusing for me.

'I am not sure there is a classification for genetic females who prefer transgendered partners. I have heard the term 'transbian', into which category I probably fit. Generally, I use the term pansexual though, in that I can be attracted to any person of any gender. I tend to be guided far more by personality than gender.'

Another woman had a different self-image but a similar perspective:

'I would have said my sexuality was straight, but when you have sexual relations with your male partner when they are dressed in women's clothes—and you seem to be enjoying it a lot—then it makes you think: "perhaps I have bi-tendencies?"'

After all this debate, my gut reaction is to claim that I am not a lesbian. If I look deeply into my thoughts, beliefs, actions, behaviours, lifestyle etc., I can comfortably conclude that I am definitely not solely a lesbian. To be crystal clear and a little graphic, I like penetrative sex with my partner's penis. I think the bigger question is, am I bisexual?

I consider this with the same line of thought as the latter woman's comments above; I do enjoy sexual situations spent with my partner dressed in women's clothing. Does that make me bisexual? I don't know. As much as I like penetrative sex, I do find women attractive. That is to say women, on the whole, can be very aesthetically pleasing to the eye.

On the other hand, with that argument, you could have the majority of women questioning their sexuality, simply for passing comment on another woman being attractive. I think the contrast is that men are not as equally willing to pass judgement on other members of their gender in the looks department, probably in fear of seeming to be gay.

Or, perhaps this is all just conjecture, and I merely cannot come to terms with my latent sexuality—I am too afraid to be out of the closet—so have I found some sort of halfway house? I will probably never convince some of you that I am anything other than a raving lesbian!

I am resigned to the fact that some people just find it impossible to get their heads around this. There was one noteworthy experience Nicci and I had together. We were going to our friend Annie's birthday meal with drinks at a pub, and there was a large group of people attending. We were some of the first to arrive. The table was a long, banqueting style one and Nicci and I sat opposite each other at one end. SJ was there already, chatting to us. Soon, another couple arrived and they were both very young (in their early twenties, I'd say). I cannot remember the boyfriend's name, but I remember that the girl was called Debbie.

SJ introduced us all and Debbie's boyfriend went to get drinks.

Debbie was left at the table with us.

'So, you're gay, right?' she said abruptly, addressing Nicci. She was obviously one of those rare but wonderfully honest people you occasionally meet in life.

Initially taken aback, Nicci remained good-spirited about it.

'No; Laura's my partner,' she responded.

This young girl then pointed to me.

'So, you're gay then?' she asked.

Now, I must have been having a particularly dim moment that evening, as for a brief moment in the bizarreness of the situation I genuinely did not know why we were having this conversation. It is so natural to me to be out with Nicci dressed as a woman. Not only that, but for our large circle of friends, our relationship is accepted with the group so sometimes I momentarily forget that it is not 'normal' for new people around us.

'No, I'm not gay,' I responded.

At this point, Debbie apologised. I'm not really sure what for, especially since she continued—wonderfully, like a fascinated child—to ask questions about the subject, apologising for each and every one, despite Nicci and I being our usual encouraging selves. In the end, I recall that Nicci had to be quite graphic in 'assuring' her that 'he' had the right equipment for us to have a very much heterosexually satisfying bedroom life, thank you very much.

Phew! It was a bit of hard work, but I think we got through well enough in the end; she seemed able to relax and enjoy herself for the rest of the evening, curiosity satisfied.

Lesbian and gay couples are more widely accepted in society than ever before, particularly in London. People can hardly muster the energy it takes to raise an eyebrow—much less do they care to do so. Despite this, I know a lesbian couple who live and work in London and yet are still very careful about showing one another any affection in public. With this in mind, there are times when Nicci and I can forget about any ideas we might have about so much as slightly brushing hands in public—at least, whenever she is dressed as a woman. We are affectionate in very trans friendly environments—and when I say affectionate, I simply mean we behave like any other happy couple do in public, not to the extent where people shout 'get a room' at us as they pass. We have taste, darling!

I always used to think that, between homosexuality and transgender, homosexuality was the harder to understand of the two states. Yet by and large, homosexuality is well and truly out of the closet, so to speak; it is widely accepted in society. By comparison, transgendered people are still very much hiding from sight. Despite this, gender is definitely starting to blur more fluidly with the passage of time. We all have a feminine and masculine side—it just depends on how far, and how often, you dip your toe into the pool of your non-predominant gender.

Take, for example, your stereotypical 'emo' boy; slim with delicate, feminine features, dabbling with eye liner and nail polish. This is certainly subtler than the look of the 80s, courtesy of Boy George. Maybe that's why it went out of fashion—it just wasn't sustainable. Nonetheless, time periods and trends have not necessarily served the trans community well, as it supports the assumption that blurring gender lines is a passing cultural fad, a teenage phase, or an aspect of gay culture. Even within the trans scene, this mistake is made; going to a trans nightclub can be like one big girls' night out—but there are always a few letches around to spoil it. Some trans girls find it difficult to fend off unwanted attention from a gay letch hoping to pick up a cheap date.

In the polar opposite environment, your average meat market club, when a large group of men are having few drinks on a Saturday night, the atmosphere is often dripping with testosterone. If one of the crowd does something outside of the expected behavioural norms, you may well hear the others call him certain stereotypical insults: 'big girl's blouse', 'sissy' and—the ultimate insult—'poof'. The implication is thus:

a male who is not one hundred per cent manly in the eyes of the group, due to unwillingness to act as 'one of the blokes', is behaving like of a gay man. Of course, with the increasing acceptance of homosexuality within our society, such an 'insult' is becoming less and less relevant.

In this very unnerving environment, it is little wonder that trans women (genetic male) in particular do not feel they have the right support network in which to come out. They get trapped in a game of conforming to the expectations of society, for fear of the reaction they might get. But is it more fear than reality? Unlike the gay community, there are very few heterosexual trans role models out there. I can think only of Eddie Izzard (who is, incidentally, a transvestite rather than transgendered). All this said, that does not mean that there is not a large number of trans people who find the issue of sexuality a challenge. For each person, both gender and sexuality can be fluid. These issues simply do not fit into convenient little boxes.

More fascinating still, this blur exists within the trans community and their partners. One woman shared this story with me: she said that one of the biggest benefits she felt from having a trans partner was the enjoyment of sharing the gay nightlife scene—she has had more than one trans relationship and her partners all preferred gay venues. What I love about my and Nicci's relationship is that, whilst we spend some time on the trans scene, we are by no means removed from the mainstream. We don't have any more or fewer gay friends than the average person and we spend most of our time with Nicci dressed as a woman with straight, cisgendered (non-trans) friends—which means we are fully integrated into society. I love this for all sorts of reasons. It exposes more people to transgendered issues; people who may not normally face them. This helps toward making trans people more accepted in the wider society.

There is nothing wrong with blurring the boundaries. In fact, I very positively encourage it. However, it does make trying to facilitate others' understanding very difficult—hence the understandable assumption that trans people are gay. Even when you know someone extremely well, the discoveries I made during the course of my interviews will always be genuinely very interesting. It is enlightening, without being shocking, to find out in what terms people think of the concept of being trans. A best friend of a trans person will still be surprised by what they hear, not least because it is complicated—very complicated. I assure you, people on the trans scene do not always agree on many aspects of it and the experience differs greatly between each individual.

I will always remember one of the first times I met SJ and how she responded to Nicci and me as a couple.

'You, I get … I think,' she said, pointing to Nicci in a restaurant over dinner. Nicci was wearing a particularly gorgeous dress we'd seen in a shop together (which I wish I'd bagged for myself). 'It's you that fascinates me!' she added, looking at me.

I didn't receive an explanation for this peculiar comment until the day I interviewed her. I was explaining my past relationship with H.

'It makes sense to me now,' said SJ. 'You left someone who was struggling to deal with his identity and you walked straight into a relationship with someone different—the type of person you wanted him to be.'

Succinctly put and essentially true. We'd had a glass of wine or two by that point (who says you can't mix work and play) if I'm honest, but what we actually said was more along the lines of: Nicci is the finished article. But of course, she isn't really—none of us will ever finish growing and changing.

SJ made the very perceptive observation that because people don't understand 'cross-dressing' [sic], it is easier to box them into the gay category.

'We have all asked you and Nicci so many questions in order to understand exactly how your situation differs from homosexuality,' she confessed.

I still haven't really answered the question of my sexuality. I don't think I can, either, if you consider all that I have said. If you start to analyse it as I have, how many of us could have some reason to question our sexuality—even in the tiniest way? I agree with other women in trans relationships: the situation you are in does make you question certain things, not just your sexuality. If these questions stay just as questions, I see that as a very positive thing. Challenge and debate is good as long as you don't let the questions concern you too much.

Overall, those around you should accept you as you are—if you are comfortable with who you are and how you live your life, the chances are that others will be too. If not, perhaps it is worth asking some difficult questions about whether or not they should be in your life.

If It's Not a ♥ Personal Question …

Once established that I am not homosexual, the spotlight whirls around and shines fiercely in my face, as the confused have an expectation of further clarity—in a desperate attempt to understand such an unusual relationship. I will always welcome the opportunity to answer questions. I want to help people understand, and they can only do this by exploring.

Having read this far, I am sure that questions (and most likely, assumptions) are spinning around your head like a merry-go-round! If you are unfamiliar with the trans scene, you may well be still trying to get to grips with what you have learned up to this point. I will attempt to tackle some of the common questions that are asked about trans relationships.

Firstly, Nicci does not dress like Lily Savage, or any other drag queen, for that matter. This is because she is not a drag queen, which is a different thing entirely. And no; she does not sneak into my knicker-drawer trying to steal the chance to dress up as a woman!

Another myth is the idea that if trans people are not drag queens, they must be hidden away behind closed doors, never venturing outside the house—after all, it would be an inconvenient challenge to society's preconceptions of gender. It is not the case; trans people integrate into society just fine and frequently enjoy good social lives.

If you have made any of the above assumptions, you have not done anything wrong. No one is a true expert on any topic and if you have never been exposed to the subject, why should you know anything about it? As with all things, it has its own set of complex nuances and etiquette. The fact of the matter is that neither Nicci's nor any other person's situation can be easily reduced into a set of rules; it just is what it is and it varies from person to person.

Not only that, but even people on the scene have made these mistakes. When I spoke to one partner of a trans woman, the impression of trans people as drag queens was classically demonstrated; she said that, before she met her trans partner Sue, she didn't know much about the trans and cross-dressing scene—only what she knew from watching Dame Edna!

So have no fear: I am not the political correctness enforcement squad here to lecture you. I am not going to beat you with the proverbial stick over how you should or shouldn't respond to trans people. I take everything in my stride and joke about it all because, frankly, anyone who takes themselves too seriously is merely dull. I am not on a crusade to convert the masses. I will, however, make it my priority to fill you in a little around the edges on the concept of transgender. Please forgive the fact that this book really only talks about trans women—male-to-female transgendered people. My personal experience only really extends to trans women, although there are a fair number of trans men (the opposite: female-to-male).

Firstly, gender and sex are different. A person who identifies as transgender will have the physical sex of 'male' and the gender identity of a 'woman'. When such a trans person dresses and presents as a woman, it is the outward expression of who he feels like on the inside. His sex, or biological genitals, might be a cock and balls but his innermost thoughts are leaning over into feminine. Therefore it might be more correct to align your perceptions of him with his sense of who he is; to refer to him as 'her' and 'she'. The reason he wears women's clothes is to show on the outside what he feels inside—so his genitals are essentially at odds with his brain. When referring to a person who does not match the profile we have constructed for them in accordance with their genitalia, we might think of them as either a tomboy or a sissy.

Human beings like to box themselves and others into categories. Life, however, is not so straightforward. It is not as simple as: so-and-so is transgendered, therefore X/Y/Z, job done; there's your description. You cannot create a new little category box and expect to understand a whole new personality type of which you were previously unaware.

There is plenty of complex thinking and science surrounding these issues. Much as I could go into it, my aim is simply to give you information within the context to my story. This should provide you a decent overview of the subject without boring you silly from all the little details. Should you wish to read up on the subject, the literature is there in abundance, but that is not the purpose of my story.

First of all, 'transgender' in this book works as an umbrella term, under which sit various more specific terms such as: drag, cross-dresser, transvestite, transsexual, and gender dysphoric (meaning to be unhappy with your gender identity). The entertainment industry has helped most of us become familiar with drag artists such as Rue Paul. The term cross-dresser is fairly self-explanatory. A transvestite enjoys dressing in clothing not normally associated with their own gender and may get a sexual kick from it. A transsexual is someone who is so unhappy with their gender that they seek medical intervention. They may wish to alter their body with the use of hormones or—to address that crude issue people wonder about—'the chop' (it is actually inversion rather than removal, and is medically known as gender reassignment surgery, among other things).

Transgender, although an umbrella term, is also a term within itself—as I already described as not pertinent to sexuality. It is not transvestism because transvestism is not really about gender identity—you could say that transvestites put clothes on to feel a certain way inside, but transgendered women put female clothes on in reverse of this: to express outwardly what they feel they are on the inside. It's the difference between doing and being. Some do not feel they are far enough along the spectrum to be considered transsexual. This is where Nicci sits.

A cisgendered female is, quite simply, a 'biological' female or a woman who is not on the trans spectrum. Language is restrictive, and terms often come only in binary forms, as is the case with gender; we will have to make do. Think about this: the very fabric of our and many other cultures' language is built on the idea of male and female; take for instance French, where inanimate objects are categorised as either masculine or feminine (but that is another discussion entirely).

How we relate to each other is sociological. It is about class, education, experience, religion and peer groups among other things. We are all a mixed bag—a complex of these things influence how we deal with different situations socially. One situation is how someone will react to their first encounter with someone obviously trans.

For example, a friend of mine (a colleague from many years back with whom I have stayed in touch) reacted in a very intellectual way when I told her Nicci was trans. She is highly intelligent and she turned the subject over and over, inspecting it and discussing every aspect of it with me, asking lots of questions. She concluded that she had the deepest of respect for Nicci for wearing whatever she wanted. This friend added that she often wishes she had the courage to dress more unconventionally than she does; the reason she doesn't, she said, is because she does consider what others would think—much as she wishes she didn't. Therefore, she was impressed that I go out in public with Nicci dressed very femininely without caring at all what others think. My friend recognised the freedom Nicci and I enjoy.

I, in turn, am very impressed and have great respect for her in how she brings up her two daughters; she is very conscious not to have society influence them. As far as I can tell, she gives them the greatest gift there is to give: choice. It is in every little aspect of their upbringing that she teaches them responsibility of every choice you make.

Her children are asked what they want for dinner—from a choice of healthy options naturally—and what they want to read; she has never influenced them about what to wear, from the time they were old enough to recognise colours and textures. When they have gone shopping, they have chosen what they want to wear. Yet, clearly they are the girly girls their mother has never really felt she was.

As far as her own dress sense is concerned, my friend confessed to me that she wished she was brave enough to dress like a man—she thinks she would genuinely be more comfortable. Just as she was telling me this, her two daughters came running into the kitchen to both show me their Disney princess costumes they had worn to a recent party, spinning and twirling all the way.

If Nicci had been given the choice as a child, she may also have chosen the princess dresses, as would perhaps thousands of trans women. If she'd had this choice, the experience of growing up pretending she was someone she wasn't would not have been so painful.

Man, I Feel Like a Woman!

I guarantee that almost every guy in the world at some point, whether he be child or man, whether it be in public or private, has tucked his willy between his legs and said: 'Look—I'm a girl!'

Assuming you are reading this and you are happy with the gender you were assigned at birth, imagine you wake up tomorrow and you look in the mirror and, if you are a woman, what you see staring back at you is a bald head, stubble on your face, a protruding Adam's apple, chest hair, in fact all over body hair and a penis. Or, if you are man, you see smooth skin, you are shorter, you have breasts and no penis. I am biased, but in my view, one of you comes off better that the other. I am making light of the assumption that a man's initial answer might be, 'result'!

Though in all seriousness; what would you think? Would you feel disgust, repulsion, panic—maybe fear? Imagine that you cannot change. You might not know what to do or how to dress. It would be difficult to explain it to loved ones and friends; you might stay silent and try and deal with yourself, knowing that it was a taboo subject.

This is what it is like every day of the lives for anyone who is not happy with the gender they were assigned at birth. Of course, it is not as sudden as overnight—they know from a very young age that something is not right. I am simply trying to shock you; to give you a glimpse of what it might be like to live the life of a trans person, even just for a second.

I posted this question on my blog and someone replied with a very moving answer:

'I'd see a familiar person—yet strangely, a true woman in all physical assets! That day I would kiss the mirror and then I would adore every second of that day, wishing I would never wake up.'

Many of us have experienced looking in the mirror and for some reason see a reflection that surprises us. For example, you may feel younger than the years have made you. You could say that this is your starting point to understanding anyone who is trans.

Our gender is one of many facets that makes up who we are as a person. It is fundamental. For anyone who is happy with their gender, it is very difficult to understand why someone would want to change. The point is, though, that they are not trying to change; they are trying to correct what must seem like a hideous, cruel mistake of nature—to take some comfort in being able to present to the world what they feel inside; that which is not obvious to others.

When I stood up to talk at the equality day Nicci and I delivered, I asked the women in the audience: do you remember your teen years—remember learning to put makeup on (probably too heavily)? You tried to keep up with fashion and trends—and maybe failed miserably. You may have thought that you looked great at the time, but you didn't know any better. I bet if you looked back at pictures now, you would cringe. What about getting your first bra and fighting with the clasp, wondering how the hell you were ever going to get to grips with it? Perhaps you flopped down on the bed in an exhausted huff, thinking 'I'll just wear a sports bra for the rest of my life.'

Over the years, it's gotten easier. If you are in your 30s or 40s, you know what clothes suit you and how to apply makeup so it looks natural. Wouldn't it be terrible if, at the age of 30, 40, 50 even, you had to go back to being that girl that has a tantrum because she can't do up a bra. You'd have to learn it all again—start afresh as though you had never learnt any of that stuff.

After I said all that to the audience, I let the silence hang in the room, just long enough for it to sink in. Then I said: that is what it is like, if you are transgendered, to come out half way through your life; you have to learn what it is like to be a woman in adulthood, not as a teenager.

What is being a woman really? OK, don't answer that—there is probably enough content there to write another book. An even bigger question is: what is it like trying to be a woman if you are biologically male?

Before trying to be a woman, it is important to experience what it might have been like to be a little girl. Little girls want to be princesses and ballerinas; Nicci, in fact, has taken ballet classes and she is good at them. She doesn't take classes as a male dancer—she is professional and wears all the traditional dancing clothes any female dancer wears. At first, this was something she kept secret from everyone else but me, but as with everything else, over time she has become more confident and therefore open about it, because she has grown to be more and more unapologetic for who she is.

Nicci explained to her ballet teacher exactly what she wanted to achieve from the lessons; that is, she did not want to learn to dance like a male ballet dancer. She wanted to learn moves, routines and dances which were very feminine in order to help her feel more like a woman overall. These lessons were intended to take her transformation forward outside of the lessons; it would help her to move in a more feminine manner in her everyday life. When I was practising ballet as a child, I would never in my wildest dreams have imagined that I would find myself sitting in the corner of a dance studio watching my partner perform—as I did when I attended one of Nicci's lessons. She is certainly better at it than I was!

Yes that's right, I was very traditionally raised as a little girly girl, so naturally, I had ballet lessons. That is, I did until I broke my foot when I was about eight—after that I never went back. This was partly because I had started to grow out of it—or grow up, I should say— literally. It was becoming obvious that I was going to grow rather tall. Although I probably have the right physical build for a ballet dancer, I am now 5'11" and it would never be possible for me to have a career in it. Darcey Bussell is taller than many, but even so, she is not close to six foot tall.

Little girls also play with dolls. I hasten to add that Nicci does not play with dolls—I was only going to say that I received my first Ken when I was starting to get a little bored with the girly dolls, owning as I did three Cindy's (two of which were ballerinas) and one Barbie. I guess I felt I had to bring a bit of testosterone to the scene. Yet, the first thing I did with Rock Star Ken was to take off all his clothes and try to put Masquerade Cindy's ball gown on him. I was bitterly disappointed and disgruntled that it didn't fit; I remember wondering why they didn't make the dresses to fit him too. Hmm ... Do you think that was a bit of a hint as to what was to come?

After getting the girly stuff out of the way, some trans women become experts in the art of womanhood. It's bizarre how someone can study how to be a woman and become more knowledgeable about the subject than women themselves; Nicci advises me on what outfits she thinks I wear well. As a result, I dress better now than I ever have. Seriously, once I got into my 30s, I thought I knew how to apply my makeup. Apparently, I didn't have a clue. It's a good job I am not a proud woman because some women might feel offended—threatened even—if their partner showed them different techniques of applying makeup. Not me—I was grateful, because the end result was better.

Think back again to when you were a teenager; you talked with your friends about the things that helped you develop into a woman. You went shopping for makeup and had sleepovers where you talked in the dark until the small hours. You might have gone shopping with your mum for your first bra, painfully embarrassing though it was. Or perhaps that was just me—I had very little to put in my first bra. If I am honest, I still have very little, but have grown to be thankful for what I have. Anyway! Trans girls are often alone in discovering what they need to know in order to become comfortable as women.

I told SJ that I was proud of Nicci because of how well she does her make up; believe me, there are trans girls who look just awful. A bit of me wants to adopt them and take them under my wing to help them look better. That sounds really bitchy and probably is, but the truth is that they need support and help to look better. When they are still in the closet, possibly hiding their big secret from friends and family, there is very little help to be found.

Many of them go too far overboard, like Nicci did in the early stages; I put this phase down to 'kid in a candy store' syndrome. When trans girls come out, they are spoiled for choice in what they can wear and it takes a while before they settle into their look—exactly like teenage girls.

Even if a trans girl successfully passes, she may live in fear of discovery. Relationships begin with a lie—or at least, a withholding of the truth. In short, she will go through every day of her life holding a huge secret within her. Life is a charade.

If one denies that one is trans, one is also wearing a mask. It is very easy for the affected person to become consumed by such a colossal secret—particularly if they are not in a supportive environment. It is easy for the fear of being found out to become debilitating to all areas of their lives: their confidence, their relationships and their jobs. I know; I saw this happen to H.

I am aware of the scale of numbers of transgender women who do not have support in becoming the woman they feel inside. It is one reason why you are reading this book.

I did not decide to write this book as an insight into a 'freakish' kind of relationship. I am in love with someone who is transgendered. This is not a sensationalist story with the types of headlines you commonly see in women's' magazines. You know the sort: 'I walked in on my husband wearing my knickers ....'

Other women who are in transgendered relationships are hard to come by. They are few and far between—at least, publicly. All of us identify with others who have a similar point of view to ourselves, so I searched for books written by women of trans partners. I was disappointed when I found very little—they all came from a perspective of 'coping'.

I understand that this is a real issue for many people who find themselves in this unusual circumstance and I am not dismissing their experience for a moment. However, I simply could not find a story I identified with. The majority of women in the same situation seem to think so very differently to me; I do not see my situation as 'coping'. I do not see myself as needing support as the partner of someone who is transgendered. I celebrate my relationship with such a person; this person whom I love and appreciate every day. I acknowledge all the beautiful benefits of this type of relationship.

I am proud of my partner and have not struggled with her being trans. Much as I appreciate and respect the many women that do, I would like there to be representation of the positive aspects that come from this kind of relationship. I feel honoured to have been introduced to other trans people and have made many trans friends. I am inspired by their bravery and strength in standing against the crowd.

Here, I must add that some women in trans relationships have not experienced my good fortune in having the full support of friends and family who are wonderfully accepting. I would wish that other women also understand the context in which many women discover that their boyfriend, partner or husband is trans. Finding out in the wrong way at the wrong time can cause a shock that is not to be underestimated.

With this in mind, imagine this confession from the perspective of the husband; the bravery and angst he would have gone through to decide whether or not to share this with the one person he loves and—surely—trusts above all others. He has to consider that she may not accept him and that he could very well be destroying his marriage.

For the remainder of our relationship after H's 'coming out', I stayed true to my word and supported him as best I could. Sadly in our case (and in many others for a whole variety of reasons), the relationship did end.

This is the reality for many trans couples. I am aware of this. I understand it and would never underestimate the extreme difficulties women would go through when having to deal with such big news. Equally, I would never judge any woman who felt she could not stay in a relationship because her partner was transgender. Although I personally did not, many women as well as transgender women may very well need extensive support networks to help them cope.

That said, this is not unique to trans relationships per se. Many people have been on the receiving end of a dropped bombshell. Suddenly unveiled information, that is so crucial to the relationship, is a difficult thing for a partner to come to terms with. Whatever the outcome, one has to search for a solution. As with all relationships, a trans relationship has its challenges—although admittedly they are somewhat more unusual!

Having acknowledged the issue in the early stages, it was not the same experience during my second trans relationship as with the first—though I appreciate that I may be in the minority here. I started the relationship knowing that the person I had chosen was transgendered, and that there would be some parts of the relationship that I would need to approach slightly differently. I went in with my eyes wide open and I will now share with you the highs of a trans relationship. I believe that the basic rules and mutual understanding Nicci and I have can be applied to—and could improve—all relationships. Nicci and I have had to be very open and honest with one another and that is something which I think others could learn from.

Living life with a trans partner honestly and unapologetically is not about making other people uncomfortable. Nicci and I do not deliberately set out to be in people's faces about her being transgender; we go about our business like everybody else. From day-to-day, I don't look at the life I have chosen and think how odd and different it might be; in fact, I don't think there is really all that much different about it. I go to work, I sleep, I eat, I socialise with my partner.

In short, I don't see it as that big a deal. What others think about what my partner is wearing does not consume my every waking moment, as it is outwardly a triviality; in the grand scheme of things does not remotely matter. People matter—love, caring, honour and respect for people matter. I do think that having this attitude helps those who come into contact with Nicci and me. We deal with it in a relaxed way.

Nicci and I cannot be responsible for how others react. We are not responsible for their opinions of trans people, nor of me as a woman who is not a lesbian but is still in a relationship with a trans woman. We are not doing it to make people feel uncomfortable. Indeed, we do not feel we are 'doing' anything consciously at all—darlings, we have more important things to concentrate on, I can assure you!

Joking aside, Nicci and I do feel we have some duty in regards to how we communicate trans issues. That is not because we think we should or must; it is not a chore. It sounds corny, but we both feel something close to a vocation that, when there is a calling, we will do all we can to help others understand, because educating leads to understanding—in turn leading to acceptance. The goal is helping trans people to integrate into society, rather than staying on the fringe as far too many currently feel they must.

We don't set out to hurt others. Probably my more relevant experience of someone close to me experiencing difficulties is my dad. Although we did have a detailed conversation about what transgender is, he sees it, or at least did when we talked, as something Nicci 'does', rather than a part of who she is. I did try and help him to understand, but nevertheless he fell quiet the only time he was in Nicci's company when she was dressed.

Of course, in starting the relationship with Nicci, I had my first experiences of outings with my partner 'dressed'. At first, I never gave much thought to these; the first several times we went out together were at trans friendly places or with friends, and Nicci acted so naturally about it all—and why shouldn't she? At this stage, she had been out for some time. I do remember her marking the first occasion by saying, just before we walked out the door of her flat, 'This is your first time of going out with your partner dressed.' I don't know if this was naivety, avoidance or (and I think this is most likely the case) but I was just so overwhelmingly OK with Nicci being trans that it wasn't even an issue. She behaved in such a relaxed way that there was nothing for me to worry about.

I asked one interviewee what type of personality she thought a woman in a trans relationship would have to have.

'You are clearly comfortable with yourself,' she said, indicating at me. 'And therefore you recognise the value and importance of this and so understand the right others have to be themselves.'

And that is where I think my and Nicci's minds meet; we are both now relaxed and enjoying the experiences of going out as a trans couple—as a normal couple.

The Pronoun Game

I f a trans person considers themselves to be a woman, it raises the question of how to refer them. It is a big question and a hot topic of conversation. People are very confused by all this pronoun business. Being in Nicci's company while she, a trans person, pushes all the 'norms' and social boundaries, forces people to ask questions that they have never previously thought of.

By and large, the important thing to remember is that a transgender woman considers herself a woman and therefore you should refer to her as 'she' and 'her' when she presents in the feminine. For me, I am conscious of people assuming I am a lesbian, so in conversation with someone I don't know well, when talking about Nicci I do tend to refer to her as 'he'.

I confess that, sometimes, I do sneakily enjoy playing with people's perceptions. On one occasion, I had arrived at a conference where Nicci was due to be presenting. Having travelled directly from work, I got there before her and was chatting to a woman. I said that my partner was one of the speakers at the event that evening.

Because I knew Nicci was presenting as a woman, I did of course use 'she' in this context throughout our conversation. Moments before Nicci arrived, I got around to telling this lady that Nicci's talk was about herself and she is transgendered. She gave the obligatory gasp of 'Oh!' in a positive way, just as Nicci walked past to greet the organisers. Nicci hadn't noticed me and I pointed her out across the room to this woman. She was amazed.

'I'd never have known she wasn't a woman, she looks fabulous!' she exclaimed. I had a rare opportunity and so took it:

'So ... while we have been chatting and I have been referring to my partner as "she", did you think I was a lesbian?' I asked. The woman took a second.

'Well yes, I suppose I had, without giving it a thought,' she said.

This kind of conversation nicely illustrates some of the more unusual moments in my life—having a partner who is transgendered.

Exceptions also occur within the trans scene, when there is sometimes a need to distinguish between trans women and a biologically born, gender-euphoric woman; a woman who is happy with what is between her legs and between her ears; as Shania Twain sang: 'Man ... I feel like a woman!' In this instance, 'cisgender' as opposed to 'transgender' will work fine—or any more casual terms, as long it is recognised that both groups of people are women.

People ask: 'What should I call [Nicci in terms of gender] ... exactly?' I usually reply with my own question, to help them think about the issue for themselves, namely: would you refer to a woman as 'he' or 'him'? The answer is no. This can be a difficult idea to put across to people who refuse to accept that a trans woman is a woman, still considering her to be a man—or, crudely, a bloke in a dress. This is when I bring out my trump card: doesn't it sound a little ridiculous to refer to the person standing in front of you in a dress, high heels, make-up and holding a handbag, as 'he' or 'him'? That for me is the golden rule. Do not call Nicci he, or refer to her as him, when she is clearly presenting in the feminine. And this is the crux of it. We have to think about which gender the person is presenting as.

'You are protective of Nicci because you are very specific in saying "she",' our friend Carol observed of me. 'I can see the discomfort on your face when others call Nicci "he"; you say you prefer them to use "she".'

The second defining gender indicator is name. To me, Nicci is, always has been and always will be just 'Nicci'. She has the benefit of a name that can be either male or female. She does, of course, have the male name she was born with—which I will not reveal in respect to Nicci. Her family only ever call her this, because it is what they are comfortable with. The only time I ever call Nicci by her male birth name is when I am in their company. I do this out of respect and because I am guided by Nicci. If she asked that all her family started calling her Nicci, my allegiance would be with her and I would consider that I was supporting her and her family in leading by example. However, I have often found that transgendered people have two names; their male and female name. The same rules apply, as for pronouns, when to use a trans person's male name and female name.

The best method is to ask the person involved. This is what Carol—a good friend of ours—did when Nicci first came out.

Carol recognises Nicci's preference for the female pronoun to be used in connection with her. 'It makes it easier for me, so I won't get confused', Carol explained. 'Nicci will now always be Nicci to me. I sort of forgot about her male birth name because "Nicci" is what she prefers.'

Regardless of how Nicci dresses, Carol sees her as 'she' because she understands that Nicci will never be offended by being called, 'her' or 'she' when in male mode—but the same cannot be said in reverse.

Carol described how, because she and her husband have known Nicci for so long and because they have discussed the issue in detail, there is trust between them, which runs deep. I could see this from the first time I met them as a couple, the day that Nicci first introduced me. They recognised and understood how much courage Nicci had when she came out to them—how incredibly difficult it was for Nicci to tell them such an important thing. Knowing how much effort it took for Nicci to say the words she needed to say, Carol wants to make everyone feel comfortable. She admits that this is not without its difficulties, she may slip up and use the male pronoun or Nicci's male birth name, and get annoyed at herself for it. For her, it makes it easier to refer to Nicci in the female all the time, regardless. She can see that we are both most comfortable with this.

'Why would I make everyone uncomfortable?' she reasons. 'I value the closeness we have—the friendship and trust that Nicci has put in me to discuss intimate things in her life. So why would I ever do anything to upset that balance?'

A more unusual fact about Carol is that, other than me, she is the only one who will correct others if they use the incorrect pronoun—she does this with genuineness, as she understands the importance of educating. It is not done maliciously or self-righteously; in fact, from my observation, it is exceptionally gentle and tentative. I actually think she cannot help herself—she couldn't possibly let such a thing slide. This is something I greatly admire, value and respect in her; she fights Nicci's corner in a way that others do not find so easy.

People struggle much more with the concept of a trans person being one person. Again, people like to categorise others and this leads to confusion in terms of naming. Nicci's friend Monica, years after Nicci's coming out, still thinks she has two personas; the male and the female. She says that Nicci has tried to explain it to her—but, Monica met Nicci when 'he' was still using his birth name, so she will always think of her that way.

The difference in understanding between Carol and our other acquaintances shows clearly. Though I have always used 'she' when quoting, it should be noted that Monica has a tendency to refer to Nicci as 'he'—even when we are talking about her dressed as a girl! It's not an easy thing to grasp.

Fear of potentially causing offence seems to be the main driving force of people's intentions. When interviewed, Annie had just the words:

'Time makes it easier,' she said. 'The more time goes by, the easier it is to understand. I am getting used to using the right name … I'm calling her Nicci more. I'm trying.'

That is all anyone can ask; that people, maybe against all their beliefs (as with Annie), have put these aside to try and understand—to be respectful enough not to judge one another. When acceptance of being transgender comes from someone for whom the concept is a stretch on their personal beliefs, it is very valuable, powerful and humbling. In fact, this kind of acceptance—the acceptance of anyone, irrespective of their transgender nature—is what we should all look to achieve in every different type of relationship we experience in our lives. I don't think that Annie realised what a very meaningful and moving thought she had shared.

I will finish with this: I have never come across anyone who is not willing to try and use the right name or pronoun; no one has simply refused to take this step and thereby ultimately refused to accept Nicci for who she is. Everyone has been willing to take that step, however difficult.

Gender Bending

In the 70s (incidentally, the very year I was born) an author named Deborah Feinbloom said that women whose partners are transgendered 'Must all have low self-esteem or be latent lesbians.' For many people, particularly women, the only exposure they have had about 'women like that' will have come from sensationalist magazine headlines; you know the ones:

'My husband wanted to become my wife!'

'He asked if we could kiss both wearing lipstick—is he gay?'

'There are three people in our marriage!'

'He is obsessed with wearing stockings!'

And of course, the old favourites:

'I found him wearing my knickers!'

'My boyfriend likes to dress in women's clothes!'

If you were to believe various stories of partners of trans women, you could be forgiven for making the assumption that all woman in a trans relationship are unhappy about the 'problems' that they have to 'come to terms' with. When faced with a woman behind these headlines, it's a different story. I tell people all about it in a matter-of-fact way—usually as part of general conversation. I don't make a big thing out of explaining it. I won't go through it timidly and hesitantly, as if I am confessing some great shameful secret.

I can see how my falling into not one, but two trans relationships might make people think I am absolutely and insanely off my rocker. SJ embellished intuitively on how cross-dressing and suchlike could be seen as 'an infringement of the roles within the relationship'.

'Women could be very insecure about their partners cross-dressing, I am sure many women would find it difficult to deal with,' she mused. 'I would imagine that a lot of women are not strong enough to realise it is not something that is disrespectful of them.'

Despite my perfect contentment with my situation, I still occasionally receive a sympathetic head tilt from those presumably holding the above perceptions. Yet it is more often the case that assumptions range through to the other end of the scale; i.e., people couldn't care less. The subject is just another fact they have learnt in their day—my personal favourite reaction was from my boss who simply said, 'That's different.'

Those who do think something of it are considerate and well-meaning in their assumptions; they sympathise. There exists a fallacy that, as a trans partner, you are 'putting up' with the situation. Really, you would be better off with a nice 'normal' man. More than better off—you deserve better than a life where you must deal with 'the public' staring and making comments wherever you go—never mind that this could be considered a fault of the public, rather than of the relationship.

I must be very feisty, mustn't I, to be prepared to leap to my Nicci's defence at a moment's notice; to defend her honour in public, like she's some damsel in distress. Sure, sometimes most of us would like someone to stand up for us but like lots of situations, it isn't always best to draw attention to yourself or a trans woman in public. Of course, I would step up to the plate if need be, but Nicci can take care of herself and more importantly, has a right to deal with any situation in the way she chooses to deal with it.

I am no doormat and I am not so desperate to be in a relationship, that I would stay in a trans relationship if I didn't want to. I am fit and healthy, in my mid-30s, 5'11", size 8/10 and sporting an inside leg measurement of 36". I have shoulder-length brown hair, green eyes and I don't think could be called unattractive (Nicci says I am beautiful but she is biased). I have never had more self-confidence, been happier and more outgoing. I am confident that, if I was single, I could date quite successfully if I wanted. I don't think I would be lonely, as I have learnt now that you can be happier and more comfortable single than in a relationship with the wrong person. I am not in my relationship out of desperation, afraid of the loneliness. I am living a great life with the love of my life.

There are, and I think always will be (in my lifetime at least), common assumptions made, as there are with all walks of life—I am not pretending that we don't all make assumptions every day about hundreds of things, but those about a trans relationship and a trans person are a little more unique. Assumptions around subject matter like this will always exist—some more humorous than others. When I asked Monica what challenges she might face if she was in a relationship with a trans woman, her instant response was:

'Losing my share of the bathroom mirror, to start with! You'd just raid each other's closets and get on with it, wouldn't you?'

That brings us neatly onto the topic of gender roles in the relationship. Though I over generalise, you know exactly what I am mean when I say that 'he' is expected to take out the rubbish and wash the car while 'she' is expected to do the shopping and pick up the kids. I suspect 'he should be the man' is what some women may think, when they unwillingly find themselves in a relationship with a trans woman. Let me tell you right now; I won't have a man take care of me. I have always prided myself on being stubbornly independent. I am not some raging feminist who says 'down with men!' I simply believe that in this day and age, self-sufficiency is the key—although, oddly enough, it took a trans woman to soften me on this point. I'll admit I do occasionally let my guard down and let Nicci take care of me. Oh, and I accept help from my dad when it comes to car mechanics, but hey, we all have a weakness!

Nicci has her masculine side, but I think people may assume that Nicci will always present in an exaggeratedly feminine way—perhaps they have in mind an exceptionally camp gay man. This perception doesn't hold up for her or most trans women at all; strangely, when I very first started dating Nicci, it was my dad who seemed most pleased with the fact that Nicci appeared to be a 'real man.' He must be more intuitive that I give him credit for; Dad pegged H as effeminate straight away, despite him being in the closet as a transvestite. When I first described Nicci to Dad (was in the army, played rugby, etc.) I could see Dad mentally ticking off the aspects of this new man in his daughter's life, leading him to conclude; 'this one's a real man'. In fact, he outwardly claimed, in the middle of a restaurant at the end of our first family meal together, that Nicci was 'better than the last one'. Ah, how early she was introduced to my dad's brutal honesty and London East End charm.

Indeed, many people's knowledge of transgender (if they even know the term) extends only to male transvestites who are assumed to be gay men getting their rocks off by cross-dressing as women. Even a trans partner I met had the idea of numerous drag artists, but after a time in her partner Sue's company, her perception was altered.

'Being able to support Sue while she does what she does certainly adds that little something to the relationship,' she explained. 'Giving her input on make-up, outfits, hair and all that is a weirdly amazing feeling. Doing this for her makes her more appreciative of me in a way that adds balance to the relationship.'

Those without this experience are more confused by it. Though accepting of my situation, Monica is my opposite; she is attracted to men at the other extreme end of the spectrum. The more able to protect her in the most caveman-like way, the better. I love the brutally honest and unapologetic way she knows what she likes and will not accept less.

'The minute they show me softness, they turn me off,' she said. 'God help me if they cry—it means they can't protect me.' While she takes off her hat to Nicci for living honestly, she would not want her 'man' to be this way.

'It's easier to accept if it's other people. I'm accepting of everybody …' Monica added. 'But I would be shocked if it were my husband. I like a masculine man who's rough and works with his hands. I've never liked pretty boys, with soft features, so if he came home and said, "I'm going to be a tranny from today", I'd be concerned.' She went on to joke that, on the other hand, if it meant him doing the dishes and housework, she'd marry him again tomorrow!

In one of the interviews I conducted, a more unusual but interesting comment I received was in relation to my identity as a partner.

'It doesn't make sense to me,' this person said. 'I want to be with a man. How do you know who you are going to be waking up with the next day? Is it a guy or a woman? When you come home from work, who do you come home to? Which person is it going to be? That's what confuses me.'

'How do you get your head around it?' is the other comment I encounter often. 'One person is one person. Which one do you love?'

The split personality of trans partners such as these is an issue for some women. I agree—which is why I don't need to get my head around it. I only ever call my partner 'Nicci' and love her as one person with all multi-facets of her personality, exactly as any other person does their partner. Some trans partners do not. They treat their partner's male and female sides as separate entities. They confess that they are cool with the trans scene and encourage their partner to dress and experiment, but heaven forbid that ever the twain shall meet. I don't mean to sound as though I am judging them for this; it is their life and they must live by their established rules. But I believe that, overall, it doesn't do much for the trans cause.

I will say the question of gender roles crops up repeatedly. What do most women want at least in the early part of a relationship? Romance! We want to be wined and dined, don't we? Well, you guessed it; so do trans girls. You might wonder how this works when you are both women …. Well, it is tricky. This first occurred to me fairly early on in our relationship, when we were in Clacton, the night before my best friend's wedding. We had just arrived, checked into our hotel and were walking along the seafront to find somewhere to eat, when we found a cosy Italian restaurant. It was quite romantic and after we ordered, a man came around the tables selling roses. Nicci was dressed as a man, so naturally the rose seller addressed Nicci when he asked: 'Rose for the lady?'

She didn't buy me a rose but after the rose seller had gone, she joked that I could have bought her one. I was a little taken aback; it had never occurred to me and I wished that I had thought of it, as it would have been such a simple, easy gesture and one which would have made Nicci feel special. I guess this is the point; isn't that exactly why we, as women, like to be bought a rose? It is romantic. It makes us feel loved, it makes us feel feminine and it is thoughtful. Don't get me wrong—I didn't mind in the slightest that Nicci had not bought me a rose; she shows me how much she loves me in hundreds of other little ways. But it would have been so easy for me to return the favour and give her a very womanly experience that she would never have had before.

In some people's mind, this may yet again raise the question of sexual orientation. How does it work when you are both women and you both want to be romanced? It has never been an issue for us, because we show each other an equal amount of affection in the way that each of us needs it—but I know that it is an issue for some women. I think the crux of it comes down to the genetically born woman wanting to be the woman in the relationship and not come second. The trans girl might be trying to catch up on a lifetime of missing out. Somewhere along the lines of communication (or lack thereof), either one of the partners in the relationship could end up dissatisfied.

But at the end of the day, I know who I am coming home to. I am coming home to my beautiful partner and I don't care if I walk in the door and she greats me in a man's t-shirt and jeans or tights, a skirt and a woman's top. It is no different to me than a guy coming home to his wife and she might be wearing jeans or a dress or even her PJs. She does not change into a different person because she had changed her outfit. When you look at it on this level, I really believe it is ridiculous to think of it in any other way; the only reason that people do so is because the issue is taboo in our society. I am not putting anyone down who does not consider it in this way—certainly not partners, as it is not as easy for some women as I find it. I am blessed by not having to add children into the mix, which of course is a separate issue relevant to trans couples.

I was pleasantly surprised by Carol's reaction when discussing how she would feel if it were her own husband.

'I think it would be a little fun!' she said. 'It is about love, and love is not about what you wear—providing there are no secrets. It's not about whether or not you wear make-up and paint your nails. It's about loving that person for who they are.'

This resonated so strongly; I hear it so rarely from other women. It would be great if more people followed Carol's example.

In contrast, SJ once joked that all our friends have asked questions like 'How you deal with sharing your handbags and shoes?' Though not meant seriously, it is actually a very common cause of genuine curiosity. The first time Nicci and I delivered a transgendered awareness session, we had to answer delegate questions.

'Do you share clothes?' was the first question out of one eager delegate's mouth. At which point, Nicci looked herself up and down. She turned to me and looked me up and down.

'Well, seeing as there is an additional 'one' at the start of my dress size: no,' Nicci replied, which was met with a great spiral of laughter from the audience. It was a wonderful way to end the session. Humour is a great educator as it sticks. When battling against others' assumptions, being yourself will usually warm people to you, as Nicci has proved just by living life true to herself.

Social Order

What is the first question anyone asks when a child is born—before it is born, even? Yes, you guessed it: 'Is it a boy or a girl?'

When parents don't want to know what their child will be, close family and relatives may wonder what they can possibly buy the new baby without knowing this information. I am deliberately not expressing this in terms of knowing what sex the child will be, as we have learnt that the relevant thing is not what sex the child is, but rather what gender it is.

At the heart of this issue is, once again, the comfort we all take from categorising—fitting something neatly into a convenient little box. In this case, if the baby is a girl, you can buy her something pink. If a boy, the traditional choice is blue. At some point, children are innocent and simply behave in a way that seems natural to them; until they were taught a heavily loaded, saturated version of our culture's expectations, learning fear from adults of the scary and hideous results if you do not act according to the 'norms'.

It is about expectations. In the complicated world we live in, these expectations are endless. There are hundreds of them placed on us and we place them on others; rules, regulations, and norms. These may vary from culture to culture, country to country or race to race but they are there in every society, developed or otherwise. They start from before the day we are born and they shape every one of our relationships. Of course, influences of upbringing and life experiences also shape us and mould who we become. However, we all fundamentally rely on certain assumed ground rules with which to run our lives.

Part of us is shaped by those we associate with and we are closest to or most intimate with. These relationships have a very big influence on the person we become; many of the decisions we make in our lives take us down a path that changes us forever. In spite of this, I strongly believe that the choices we make fundamentally boil down to either fear or love. This concept is at the core of this book and I stress that it is a personal belief, which you may or may not agree with. Actually, the thought was first planted in my mind when I watched the film Donnie Darko (an excellent film, I might add). Although Donnie Darko himself was none too keen on the idea, it spoke to me and made sense. If one were to think about it, I am sure that in any given crossroads in life, whatever decisions made (or not made), could relate back to either fear or love. This begs the question: where and when do we learn to operate from a position of fear?

I believe we are all destined to have a particular personality at birth. If we were able to formulate the thoughts, reasoning and intellect, we could claim; 'I know who I am'—in terms of knowing the person you were meant to be and deserving to be loved. Every child deserves to be loved. It is a crucial part of our development. It helps us heal when we are unwell. Loving encouragement from parents drives our achievements at school.

Yet even in this infant stage, where we know we deserve love and demand it, this feeling is short-lived; sooner or later, we will be chastised by a parent or guardian. This chastising, whilst necessary for disciplinary purposes, hits us at a very early stage of our development, and as a result we are influenced to question our behaviour and actions. We are set parameters and taught to meet conditions—in this way, we learn that there are expectations to meet in order to earn love from our parents. We learn to fear loss of love if we do not behave a certain way. This we take into adult relationships—but in an adult-to-adult relationship, true love should be unconditional and we must be free to become the person we knew we were supposed to be. Overcoming our social conditioning is the ultimate challenge.

Following on from the subject of expectation, we have all learned how to interact and behave in relationships from our parents, guardians or primary caregivers. We take these relationships into adulthood and all usually want our loved ones to have the best of everything, to be happy and—particularly in partnerships—we often hope that we are the best person to give our partner all they need. In honesty, we hope that as the relationship grows and you give more of yourself, the same treatment will be returned to us. To some extent, we will develop into who we are as a result of absorbing aspects of those around us—a sort of social osmosis. In some relationships, even an adult-to-child relationship, this can be very destructive.

I would like to illustrate the power of expectations and societal norms, consider this: in the mid-60s a woman gave birth to twin boys, but one of her sons tragically lost his penis during a botched circumcision. As a result, the medical professionals decided to surgically reassign John to Joan. It was considered a case of nurture over nature; Joan would be raised as a girl and would be perfectly content. However, in reality Joan never felt comfortable as a girl. When he approached adolescence, he refused to continue taking female hormones and instead transitioned back to living as John—the person he felt he had always been.

I am sure that everyone who was involved in making the decision at the time thought that they were doing what was the best for John— the medical professionals and his parents. I am equally sure that Great Ormond Street Hospital, who were still operating on children to assign their gender at birth as late as 2007, felt that they were acting in the children's best interest handing these children a second chance. It was supposedly simple; they would measure the phallus (penis or clitoris) of children for whom the sex was mixed or ambiguous. If it was oversized, the child should be a boy; undersized, a girl. Of course, they could know nothing of those individuals' eventual gender dysphoria.

Admittedly, those are extreme examples, but they illustrate the magnitude of strength in our belief of black and white and how our society strives to tick all the right boxes for the purposes of fitting in. From now on, when next you fill out a form—any form, for whatever reason—notice which questions it asks. You'll notice it asks for your sex or gender, as one option. I'm willing to bet that there will also be only two choices: male and female. No 'undecided' and rarely a 'prefer not to say'.

Our perception of gender seems largely based on trivial aspects of ourselves. We have built gender expectations on what we wear and as such, clothing is the primary tool transgendered people have at their disposal. Yet our society has deemed that men do not wear skirts and dresses. The greatest accolade for any trans woman is to 'pass' in public; to dress as a woman and have no one question if they are a man. I find it astounding that, with all the scientific advancements and technological improvements humans have made to improve our lives, we are still so backwards on such a relatively simple issue as the clothes we wear.

Gender shouldn't matter—but it does; it matters if the gender you were born with is incongruent with that which you feel in your mind. It shapes how you perceive yourself. Imagine that you had to describe yourself to an alien; I bet you would include your gender. Gender matters, because in our society it shapes others' expectations of you—but it shouldn't count as long as you are being true to yourself. It takes a huge effort to deeply hide who you are. Nicci's view, now that she is open and honest about being transgender, is that there is nothing wrong with her; it is others' expectations, and society which needs to change its views.

'There is no traditional box,' a friend told me. 'While the majority of people go through their lives blissfully unaware of this, Nicci has discovered it. That's why I appreciate her company, he is not trying to be anyone she is not. What you see is what you get and he will say it as he sees it. But he makes it very clear that this is just how he sees it, and everyone is entitled to their different views.'

Social roles are extremely powerful, and whether we like it or not, we all live by them—though it may be to a different degree depending on your lifestyle. I would imagine that some people think that Nicci and I live by them to a much lesser extent! However much you live by them, they are there all the time and we are imprisoned by them; there can't be that many people flying against the torrent of daily winds forcing us in one direction.

With this background of expectation, is it any wonder that so many of us fall into relationships littered with unspoken expectations? After a time the romance will cool and then we start to pick at and overturn the loose soil on which we have grounded the relationship. Wherever there are partnerships based on faulty expectations, disappointment inevitably sets in.

I have come upon the personal conclusion that the expectations we place on our adult romantic relationships stem from childhood. Count how many little girls you've met who, when given the opportunity to dress up, choose a wedding dress. So many are over the moon to be asked to be a bridesmaid, dreaming of the day when it will be their turn.

The fascinating side of this is that children have an innocent way of just being themselves and not caring what anyone thinks—we have so much to learn from them! When it comes to freedom, they can teach us so much more than we can teach them. It occurs to me that all we teach them is how to fit in—which in a roundabout way teaches them what is frowned upon. They learn the fears of adults. If it were a young boy who wanted to be the same bridesmaid, it becomes an issue. It is due to parental fear of what other people will think, not only of the child, but of the parents themselves for 'allowing' the behaviour. As a result, the child learns to conform.

Now a transgendered child may be a more unique example, but they are really no different from any other child who may feel that there is something different about them. They are not blank slates to be written on, but have a strong sense of their true identity at a very early age. However, from the thousands of behavioural signals they get from adults, they learn not to reveal that identity. They learn to pretend to be who they are expected to be. They learn not to say the 'wrong thing'. They learn to keep secrets that they know they can never reveal. So they go on quietly living a life burdened by feeling alone and confused in an unsupportive world. They may never show any of this outwardly, and may even be the most popular kid at school; thereby perpetuating the myth of being 'normal'.

My point is this: our society does this to all of us. We even do it to ourselves. We adapt our behaviour to meet the expectations of others. We do it to each other in our relationships and we pass it on to our children to start the cycle again. It's time to break free!

I am not asking for you to be a hero and join a radical organisation. You don't have to stand on a street corner with a placard, pledging allegiance to your beliefs. Just have the courage to question whether you are really living the life you want, as the person you want to be and to be brave enough to let your children discover who they are, uninhibited; despite how difficult it might be for you to handle. I believe if you decide to have children, then that is just another one of the responsibilities you must take on.

Natural vs Normal

Questioning our current perceptions of gender opens up a can of worms in regards to right and wrong. I must ask: what do right and wrong really mean? When I interviewed our friend Annie she said 'A man is a man and a woman is a woman.' She added that if she had to deal with a husband who came home and shared the fact that he was trans with her, she would divorce him. It was the way she was bought up and in her religion, the idea of changing one's sex is wrong. While she is willing to accept trans women for they are and won't judge them, for her being in a relationship with someone trans would be an absolute no-no.

But irrespective of religion, the concept of right and wrong is so subjective. They are loaded with our personal background, upbringing and cultural heritage. There is no one true definition. Mine would be 'whatever floats your boat as long as no one is getting hurt', and this perception is shared by many others. However, it is not as simple as that. The crux of it comes down to the individual. It is about someone's personal values and who they are. That said, these are mostly derived from what was discussed in the previous chapter; how often do any of us really question what we know, or the values we have lived by, and examine them to see if we could have been misguided? We could be making uninformed decisions to categorise something as wrong, when it is not necessarily anything of the sort.

I challenge you to pick one of your beliefs, research the subject, pick it up, turn it over, look inside it as you have never done before. Are you even willing to agree that you can see how, from someone else's perspective, they can believe the opposite of what you do, just as strongly? You may not even be the same person now as you were before you made your initial conclusion. Events that transpire in your life will slowly shift your views, until you are no longer really the person you thought you were. Your schooling, religion, others' influence and suchlike may have taught you *not* to think for yourself on certain subjects—to think that such-and-such is simply wrong. Most importantly of all; are you denying your true self as a result of this?

What we do not understand, we fear. Historically, when the human race is threatened, it fights; we shoot first and ask questions later. Previously, I mentioned John, who lost his penis in childhood. He was denied growing up as a little boy. He was plunged into what I can only imagine was a dreadfully lonely, deeply sad childhood because all the adults—his parents, the medical profession, sociologists and society itself—all believed that the right thing to do was to raise him as a girl. As humans, we think we know better, but the fact of the matter is that we don't always.

I was in a relationship when I started to have feelings for another person and my beliefs were that it was wrong to do anything about this. I was committed to my then partner. But the real issue was not cheating; it was that we had grown apart and I told myself that the reason I should not leave the relationship was because it is wrong to leave your long-term partner because the length of time you have invested is a commitment in itself. I kept believing this, even though nothing else about the relationship fitted.

In discussions about my partner being transgendered, the word 'normal' is often used in order to distinguish my relationship from those of others. Once used, it is very hard to get away from it. During my interview with Annie, the word 'normal' was used early on, and from that point on in the conversation it seemed to become increasingly difficult to avoid. We ended up in fits of giggles as we challenged each other not to use it—at which point, it became impossible. This started from her asking me if I had ever been in a 'normal' relationship. She then immediately hit the nail on the head and asked 'But what is normal anyway?' This is exactly my point—yet we all use 'normal' as a description. Try as we might, we cannot get away from it.

A trans partner replying to my online questionnaire described one of the problems she felt were faced by women in trans relationships. This was the fact that 'there is still a huge amount of discrimination and taboo, i.e. that it's not 'normal' or it is 'perverted'. Take away the sexual connotations of this word, and the Oxford Dictionary definition of 'perverted' is: 'leading away from what is natural or acceptable'.

This woman reached a certain level of comfort when she realised 'We are just normal people'. I am sure that, quite often, outsiders must think women like me are mad; we have the option of a nice 'normal' life and we choose trans relationships. I have to say that I don't feel my life is so extraordinary—it is just that it is perceived this way by people who don't generally understand and know me very well, particularly when I first tell someone that my partner is transgendered. I am fortunate that I have not experienced this, but I have read stories from other women who have; a trans partner might be blamed for her choice to be such. I am very accepting and supportive, and this could be open to others' disapproval, as though as 'his' partner, I have some responsibility for 'allowing' this abnormal behaviour.

Personally, I don't believe in 'normal', I believe in 'natural'. I live my life in a way that is natural to me. Nonetheless, we live in the society we live in. I know that my partner and I are in the minority and that our relationship is what you could call 'a love less ordinary'. Others do live by the generally accepted rules of right, wrong and 'normal'. Nicci and I do not fit into these. While I may have a laissez-faire attitude, I have to acknowledge that we cannot behave in public as other couples perhaps can, so we are forced to buy into the very fabric of society's make-up—something which I fundamentally disagree with.

I often get comments of how brave I am, and how strong. I am not so sure that I am; not when you consider the adversities some people have to live through—trans women themselves, for a start. People are acknowledging me as a rebel and the 'bravery' they refer to is my living a life that is outside of the 'norms', but I am only on the sidelines. It is Nicci who has to face the limelight, the stares, the nudges and winks. This is part of what makes me so very proud of her, particularly in public—she is beautiful and brave and has the courage to step outside and show the world she won't let preconceptions stop her being her own person. In this way alone, she is giving to the trans cause. Perhaps, more significantly, she and every other trans woman are showing everyday people that it is possible to fight through preconceptions, because the battle just to be you is deeply important. I believe each of us deserves to win it.

Asking Monica how she thought the families of women in my situation would take the news of a partner being transgender set her off laughing.

'It depends who they vote for,' she said. 'It's about their background, how were they bought up. There were certain things my father bought me up with in those days, like non-interracial dating, but I would like to think my family would support me nonetheless, whatever the circumstance.'

Interestingly, my dad is the same generation, and I know he would also not like the idea of my dating interracially. I don't think it is a race issue; I think it is about parents wanting their children to keep certain traditions of their upbringing, the prime example being parents who organise arranged marriages. Additionally, I think there is a real wish for difference; not doing what your parents expect of you when you grow up seems to be a driving factor for many.

On the other hand, some people are incredibly bound by parental expectation. One partner of a trans person I spoke with on a chat room told me frankly that, if they found out about the relationship, half their family would disown the pair of them.

'They were bought up in a different era, with a very strict upbringing that involved the church; this causes us a lot of trouble. We would both love to tell our respective families but at the end of the day, it's just too much hassle—as far as we are concerned, the only people who need to know are those it affects: just me and my partner.'

What seems clear at this point is that ideas of gender are restricted to time, place and circumstance—not morality. I have what some might call very old fashioned views for someone my age, but nonetheless my principles have always been to do 'the right thing'; in this case, the right thing by your partner. You are meant be loyal and honour your unity. What my deeply held views did not encompass was the concept of doing the 'right' thing for yourself; something which I now consider to be equally if not more important. This does not amount to selfishness; it means only that you are also a person who deserves as much consideration as the next. It just goes to show that 'right and wrong' are not clear-cut concepts that are workable in everyday life.

In view of people's different levels of understanding, I have to dedicate a section to a very special friend—someone with whom I have a shared journey in a way; her journey of coming to understand and accept Nicci being transgender. For me, many of us could serve well from taking a leaf out of her book—not just in understanding the concept of being trans, but also her attitude of willingness to accept people for who they are. I am talking about Annie, for whom the idea of being a trans partner would never be acceptable for her.

She is a gentle happy soul who has very definite religious beliefs about what is right and what is wrong. Yet, I never knew that she had these beliefs until I interviewed her for the book. This is testament to her being the kind of person who would never ram her beliefs down your throat.

Annie is rather famous amongst our friends for her initial reaction to Nicci's coming out as trans. After a period of quiet reflection, she burst out with 'But … you've got a penis, so you're a guy!' Annie was reminded of this many times over the years in warm friendly jibes—she was never allowed to forget it! In any case, it is my perception that she became somewhat of a convert towards the idea of Nicci being trans.

When I interviewed her, she confessed to me that when everyone was out as a social group, she tried to distance herself from Nicci because she was not comfortable. Annie didn't want to spend too much time with her.

She felt that she wouldn't want to introduce Nicci to her friends or others she knew, in case she was judged by others for being associated with Nicci. In particular, she didn't want to be put in the situation of introducing Nicci to friends who she thought might not be comfortable with Nicci being trans.

'I worry what strangers in the pub think of me being with Nicci. I know I shouldn't but I do', Annie confessed.

I found this honesty and the revelation of the inner battle she was having very moving. Interestingly, she said it was easier if I was in the group with Nicci because of my openness. After some probing questions, I found out that for her it came back to the issue of homosexuality, though if I was with Nicci as her partner, there was less speculation about this. Just to give a little context, Annie is from abroad and as such has a very different cultural background to that experienced by people in England.

'Sometimes when I am in Nicci's company, I want to back away; I need space to get comfortable with it.'

Gradually she became more comfortable with it.

'I always feel I am offending Nicci by using "he" and "she" at the wrong times but I am getting more used to Nicci now,' she said. 'I see him as a guy because I met him as a guy, so when I refer to him and think of him, it is as "he".

'Time makes it easier to understand, not accept; I am OK with Nicci but I don't accept the trans aspect of him. The more time goes by, the more I slowly understand and I am getting used to using the right name.'

I made a promise to everyone I interviewed for the book that what we talked about was confidential. Annie has since agreed for me to share this story, but at the time I found this interview difficult; when we were next together as a group of friends with Annie and Nicci both present, I was obviously very conscious of what she had confessed to me. I was protective of Nicci and I didn't tell her about the specifics of the interview. The knowledge of what was said between me and Annie allowed me to subconsciously observe her behaviour.

I had little cause to worry—shortly after interviewing Annie, I saw her quite quickly warm towards Nicci. I could observe it as a bystander, after our conversation. I saw a barrier lift and she became more open with Nicci, greeting her literally in a more physically friendly way. I was relieved and immensely pleased that I could have perhaps influenced just one person's understanding—not least someone so important to me.

However, Annie went beyond this. On one occasion I had bought a beautiful dress for Nicci's birthday. I was passing the café Annie worked in and so I popped in to show her, and she took genuine interest and even helped me wrap it, with no discomfort whatsoever, as though this had always been the most natural thing in the world. In fact, I would go so far as to say that she has completely come around as she had a hand in educating someone else about Nicci's situation; Brian, a work colleague of Annie's who had only met Nicci as a guy before that point, but knew she is transgendered.

'Nicci came into our workplace one day dressed very simply; plain skinny jeans with a dress over the top, nice hair and make-up,' Annie recounted. 'Brian came out and started to serve her. Just then, he realised who she was. He came out the back to me in a panic and said "I don't know how to treat him!"

'I told him he must treat her normally—but then he started asking "What am I supposed to do—what am I supposed to say?" I replied that he should just relax and treat her just as he would usually treat her—as he would treat any other customer.

'After Nicci left, Brian was very cool about it. He said "She is no different to usual; just a few more girly attributes and a slight difference in voice."'

Sadly, Annie has now moved back to her home country. I spent her last night in England with her trying to enjoy as much of her company as I could before she left. I reminded her of our interview and said how much respect I had developed for her as a result. When I highlighted this, she jumped in.

'I know, I was really surprised too,' she said. 'I felt much more at ease—I enjoyed being with Nicci so much more after that.'

I replied that it had been obvious how much better she felt; she was different with Nicci so soon after, and they seemed much closer as a result. Annie added that she had understood more about how difficult it could be being Nicci, and tried to see what life must be like from Nicci's perspective. Their relationship improved so much that Nicci was the last person to see Annie before she left the country, as she saw her off the next day at the airport.

For me, this story perfectly illustrates one person's journey of understanding, accepting and integrating trans people into their lives—and how many other people could also change their perspective.

(S)expectations

There are a number of reasons why a trans relationship can be a beautiful thing. The first that springs to mind (as I have said countless times) is that it is, in a nutshell, 'the best of both worlds'. Perhaps it would be more accurate to say; 'it is the best of all possible worlds'; he can be a man when I want: protective, strong, everything I want him to be in the bedroom. She talks and listens—and I mean really listens; she will engage in the conversation more, she will remember things I have said and pick up on it later in another conversation at another time.

Equally important is that I have never been interested in 'real men'. Pauline, a friend of mine and a partner of a trans person herself, fell into relationships with trans women for reasons seemingly very similar to mine. I must stress there was no conscious aim for either of us to bag ourselves a trans partner, it was just that neither of us was attracted to your typical alpha male. I cannot think of a more hideous nightmare of a relationship than to be stuck with some beer-swilling, football thug/lad type. Both of us were more attracted to feminine-type men. I don't know if we gave off some undetectable vibe that trans women could sense, but I am inclined to think there is no rhyme or reason to our relationships; we both unintentionally started relationships with men who turned out to be trans and found that we loved this type of relationship. Yes, that's right—I am not the only weirdo! I hear you thinking it. It's all right. I've said before I am highly unlikely to be either surprised or offended.

Beauty is in the eye of the beholder. As difficult as I am sure some will find this to understand, I am just as attracted to Nicci when she is wandering around fresh from the shower spritzed with Izzi Myaki aftershave as I am when she has just pulled on knickers, tights and a bra from the drawer.

'I can't even wrap my head around it,' a friend told me, referring to my and Nicci's sex life. 'When he is he, it must be normal; when he is dressed as Nicci, it's too much to think about!'

We all know that biologically, men and women are physically different from each other. Therefore, when men and women become intimate together, they are both exploring somewhat foreign territory. Part of the excitement, I would agree, is getting to know what both of you like; where to touch to give that electric feeling, how to stroke to send them into ecstasy. Yet, how many times have you read a book, magazine article—else held or overheard a conversation (usually between women)—about a dissatisfying sex episode? Firstly, let me just get this out of the way; if you have not told the man in question what, where and how you like to be touched, then you have nothing to complain about. Men are not mind readers. Oh, and it's the same in reverse as well, lads. Come on people: communicate!

Some transgendered women love the female body. You could say they study it in order to emulate it. Transgendered girls spend so much time trying to achieve the same form and feeling of womanhood that they see around them every day—a feat which may take a lot of dedication. In my experience and from conversations with others, I have noticed that when trans women are with a woman, they lavish her body with extravagant and exquisite attention to detail. They are explorative and bordering on worshipful. Somehow, they appreciate what you are feeling because they try to understand as best they can, how it would feel if it were them.

Just imagine for a moment how pleasurable this could be! Every time you make love to your partner, there is a dance of passion; they are touching you in all the places you want to be touched, taking you to dizzy heights of sensation you never thought possible; perhaps in a way which you have never before experienced from a man—even doubted that he could give you that intensity of feeling. Although I have advocated explaining your wants and needs, I have personally found that I don't need to; apparently, it is instinctual to Nicci. I don't have to ask— I just get.

How does it feel? It's like someone has reached into your head and knows exactly what you want, gives it to you willingly without expecting anything in return and genuinely gets as much pleasure from giving to you as you are from receiving.

My experience of making love to Nicci is breathtakingly beautiful. It makes me feel like the sexiest, most attractive woman in the world and it's a massive confidence boost that makes me want to return all the pleasure. It is the closest you can possibly feel to another human being; the closeness I feel towards my partner is indescribable. The love it makes me feel in the moment is literally beyond words. I am not one for gushing romance and some of you may find this a bit nauseating—but is it hard to describe in any other way. When we make love it is overwhelming in the most delicious way you can possibly imagine.

I am tentative about how much of our physical relationship to share with you but I think it is important to explore in order to give a fully rounded picture of my experience in a transgendered relationship (I stress once again not a transsexual relationship). I believe that, generally, women and the female form are more aesthetically pleasing to the eye than the male. A lot of the fabrics women wear are very tactile and in the bedroom using certain fabrics can be very sensual; silks, satins and nylons gently stroked over your naked partner can be very pleasurable and will spice up your sex life. With this in mind, I urge all couples to experiment. Wear knickers and tights, or for me a bra does the trick, too. I promise you, if you can cast aside any preconceived connotations that come with these types of clothes and simply enjoy the feel of the fabric as you both roll around the bed kissing passionately, you will enjoy it immensely. How many of you women have had your boyfriend wear your knickers ... or else know a friend who has? Come on, be honest! If you genuinely haven't tried it at least once, then trust me: you are missing out.

I realise some women reading this may prefer a man to be a man in the bedroom; to be rough, tough and strong. Well, let me tell you ladies ... you can have both! Welcome to my greedy world of having it all, whenever I want it.

It may only be a trivial matter—and Nicci will kill me for sharing this with you, so shhhhh, we just won't tell her—but ladies, just think about how annoying it is when your man pees all round the toilet seat instead of hitting the target. Disgusting! I don't have to put up with that, because not only does my partner pee sitting down—because she's a woman—but she also cleans the whole bathroom for me. Boasting, moi? Too right; it's a pleasure I will never cease to appreciate! Ah, domestic bliss. I think there is merit to the theory that we are attracted to something we see in ourselves. Perhaps I see more of myself in Nicci because I am a very feminine woman in every clichéd way you can think of. Hey—tone it down! I don't mean 'Barbie' feminine!

Speaking of Barbie brings me neatly onto clothes shopping. A good friend, whose partner is trans, described her thoughts on the relationship. Aside from having a very understanding partner, she talked about how so many of her friends are dissatisfied with their relationships because, they say, 'men don't understand women'. They feel they are true golf widows, or football widows (or insert your own partner's frustrating hobby here); those poor individuals whose partners never want to go shopping or accompany them doing 'girly' things. With a partner on the same gender spectrum as Nicci, you generally don't have that problem. Certainly, both my friend and I have someone who is always willing to go shopping with us. The only problem is that she often can't drag her partner out of New Look's shoe department.

In my and Nicci's case, it's a wonder we ever get away and that the staff don't find us asleep on the shop floor when they open the store in the morning—surrounded by shoes, lovingly clutching a pair we've have taken a fancy to in fear someone might dare wrestle them away from us, sleep-dribbling onto the heel. It brings a whole new image to Sex And The City's Carrie Bradshaw's fantastic drawling line for when she sees a pair of shoes, falls in love with them and simply must buy them: 'Hello, lover!' In fact, I remember one time when Nicci saw a beautiful pair of purple peep toe velvet shoes and joked that she was thinking of having an affair. I am conscious I am straying into dangerous obsessive territory here, so time to move on swiftly, I think. Put the shoes down and back away slowly.

On one occasion, we were shopping in the women's department of a dress shop on the high street and, once again, Nicci and I both had our eye on the same piece of clothing—this time a particular top. There was a woman hovering nearby who was also interested in this top, so she turned to us and asked if we thought it would suit her. Nicci proceeded to tell her all the ways in which she thought this woman could wear it; with skinny jeans or leggings and how a big wide belt would look good on her—that at the front of the store, we had seen some really good costume jewellery which would finish the look off wonderfully.

The woman was very grateful. She mentioned that her friend was over on the other side of the store and impatient to leave—being as she was not very good at helping anyone decide on the right clothes. Sometimes, this woman added, all you wanted was someone else's opinion.

At this juncture, Nicci joked that what she really needed was a trans partner. She laughed, agreed wholeheartedly and turned to me to say how lucky I was.

I am lucky; I know I am and I feel lucky. Every day I am thankful for the unique (and therefore special) relationship we have and the happiness it brings me. And I believe that a lot of this stems from simply getting on with living my life; no-one should live by anyone else's expectations or what society tells you is the best recipe for success—which, it seems to me, often leads to a miserable life rather than one of honest happiness. The previously-mentioned friend places a similar value on the relationship as I do, and says that trans partners have a far more caring attitude than alpha males. You can really talk to them when you have a problem, in the same way as you might with your girlfriends. In effect you get a boyfriend/partner/ husband—delete as applicable—and a female best friend, all rolled into one.

Not everyone quite sees this point of view (usually due to their own personal preferences) but still see value in how we operate.

'I don't know how the hell you do it ...', SJ once said to me, laughing spiritedly. 'But I have always been able to ask both you and Nicci, honestly, whatever I've wanted to know—because you are both so open. And not just about trans stuff—about everything!'

SJ thinks my and Nicci's partnership is wonderful in lots of ways: 'It's like having a best friend you can get pleasure from!' she concluded.

In my experience, a big advantage to my and Nicci's relationship is the blissful freedom of total honestly and openness in public. Once you have shared your biggest darkest secret, nothing is taboo. Indeed, the ease with which Nicci and I communicate is evident to me and others have observed it—even Annie, who perhaps had the most difficulty understanding and accepting the relationship, by the end of the interview expressed (in a manner that felt to me like we'd had a major breakthrough) that she too could see we enjoyed the best of both worlds.

'You get the nice part of having a girlfriend who will go shopping with you, be honest with you and tell you what is going to look good,' she said. 'And when you have sex, you still get the penis. So you've got the bedroom part which is nice, plus the girlfriend who you can share anything with and can tell anything.'

I agree with this; for me, Nicci's considerateness stands out. I believe every relationship can have this level of respect—if one is willing to work at it. There will always be ups and downs.

One time, Nicci bought a new iPad. Happy as a child with a new toy, she naturally wanted to play with it. So she spent all evening head buried in it and there was very little conversation between us. Frankly, I'd had a hard day at work and was equally uncommunicative. I did say a few things to her and got no response because she was engrossed. Eventually I went to bed leaving her to it with a brief goodnight kiss. As a scenario, I would imagine it is fairly common. You can change the specifics to fit a couple's particular circumstances. Equally, the reaction may be different.

The next day at work I received a phone call from Nicci, just to let me know that she loved me and wanted to hold me and make love to me when I got home. That thought got me through the rest of my day at work and when I got home, we made love and then got on with the rest of our evening. Much later on I started to talk to Nicci about my previous day at work, eventful as it was. She interrupted me and asked me to wait. She turned off the TV and shut down her laptop.

'Let's go to bed and you can tell me all about it,' she suggested. 'Seeing as I was such a prat last night—not paying you any attention.'

She wanted to give me that attention, full and undivided.

I think this is a prime example of how what could be an effort becomes effortless if you are both committed to having a certain type of relationship and behaving in a certain way towards one another. If you make more of a meal of it than needs be, it isn't sustainable, and eventually you may come to resent the person. You resent all the things you do for them simply because you think you ought to. I don't think that Nicci's act of acknowledgement, understanding and tender loving care is unique to our relationship—and certainly not simply because she is trans. I think it is just about knowing your partner and knowing what they would appreciate.

The elements specific to trans relationships are just a small part of the thing as a whole. The main issue is the person themselves and who they are: their beliefs, values, passions; everything they want to experience or achieve in life; those things that are most important to them. Then there is the joy of sharing all of this. It is about the delicious unfolding of your deepest essence—from one person to another; the passage of time as you get to know them more and love them more deeply with each stage of your relationship. What I love about Nicci, at the very heart of it, is not that she is trans. It is that being trans is part of her personality. I love how she enjoys this side of her, plays with it, grows to love it and become more comfortable with it with every passing day—just as all of us learn to grow into ourselves and accept ourselves over time.

After explaining the sex that I enjoy with Nicci, I usually get a very positive reaction from women. I say women, because it has only been women who ask. They, too, see that I have what a huge number of women want; I enjoy gentle and sensual touching and caresses from my lover. I am not suggesting for a minute that this is not possible outside of a trans relationship, but the majority of women to whom I have described the sex and foreplay I enjoy have replied with something along the lines of: 'That must be nice …'—very much implying they have not had that experience with the men they have had sex with.

But, come on; at this point, I want you to be honest with yourself … it's OK, you don't have to tell anyone. I won't expose you. Just be honest; if you were previously new to the subject, what were your assumptions of what happened in the bedroom between a woman and her transgendered partner before you picked up this book and (hopefully) I started to educate you?

Mindful as I am of your possible discomfort, I shall now unburden you. People do consider there must be an involvement with strap-ons, surely? This will stem from the assumption that a trans woman will have definitely had 'the chop', in which case one might not be able to conceive of any other methods of sex between the couple. Well, hopefully, if this is what you thought (no judgement if you did) I have dispelled this myth for you.

It may be this way in some trans relationships, but certainly not all. The bottom line is, you can't generalise; I would imagine it depends on whereabouts the trans person is on the spectrum. As I have described, Nicci and H are on different areas of the spectrum and as such, these sex lives were very different.

Now, I am not going to go into detail about my sexual relationship with my partner. I am not going to tell you whether we do or do not use any toys within our love life. But, with Ann Summers shops on the high street, a little bit of kinky sex in everyday couples' sex lives has become more mainstream, irrespective of other, perhaps more unusual, dynamics of the relationship. On that note, I shall leave you with a quote from one of my interviewees:

'Strap-ons aren't just for trans relationships, you know!

A Touchy Subject

N ow that we've got fake appendages out the way, I should probably talk about past experiences. Though much has changed and improved, the sort of bedroom bliss I now come to expect has not always been my experience. For my previous transvestite partner, trying to achieve the female persona took precedence over physicality. In short, wearing the clothes was more important to him than our sex life, which in the end was non-existent. In retrospect, I can see that he very much fell into the role of the public's perception of transvestites; French maids, high heels, other erotic outfits, all in the aid of reaching sexual gratification. I am not judging; it's just that in my case, it meant me not getting my rocks off and in retrospect was very unhealthy for me in the relationship. This was in complete contrast to the love-making I enjoy now (thankfully!). Of course, H and I had sex at the beginning of the relationship, but over the years, my role dwindled and dwindled until it seemed even my participation wasn't required at all.

My initial attraction to H was, as always with me, that he was not like other men in that boisterous way. He was gentle, intelligent, good-looking and I was very young and had limited experience. I had no previous sexual encounters before H as I had 'saved' myself for when I was in a relationship with someone I loved. I believed that over time, couples naturally had less sex but I genuinely didn't think it mattered.

I know now that I had never had mind-blowing sex. I didn't know how good it could be, which meant that I didn't know what I was missing, so naturally, I thought that I wasn't missing much. As long as we were together and in love, my young self thought that was all that mattered. What I didn't appreciate was that my attitude in this respect was very convenient for him because it meant that he did not have to deal with any potential problem. I don't want to say that I was brainwashed, as this would absolve me of all responsibility and that wouldn't be right—but I came to these conclusions following conversations with H. It was he who said sex was over-rated, and society was obsessed with it and its importance. I think I bought into this concept so readily because it helped me justify the fact that we did not have sex.

Instead, his ever-increasing alternative desires turned me from a doormat into a (not very good) practising dominatrix. I did this simply to be involved in some way—in any kind of act that you could call sexual. This is a prime example of how I lost myself during that relationship. I lost sight of the concept of just saying no, so desperate was I to find some platform that could conceivably be called a sex life. I tried so many different things, hoping one of them would satisfy H but nothing I tried—even at his request—did.

The simple fact was that I could never be good enough to match the fantasy in his mind. Increasingly, he withdrew into his own mind to reach pleasure; hence why I describe my involvement as unnecessary. In this way, I experimented with a few things I regret and lost some of my dignity. In the end, my partner had no respect for me in his quest for deriving some satisfaction that would not involve him needing to deal with his issues about sex. I believe that, at the time, he was psychologically unable to perform—and indeed, lacked the desire to resolve this.

Like most things that involve two parties, it works both ways. I recognise my responsibility in not communicating my feelings. As much as I think H acknowledged and dismissed my needs and wants in favour of desperately finding some pleasure for himself, I had given up on what I wanted, so therefore did not raise the issue with him. However, when he was presented with the prospect of my leaving him, he made all sorts of promises of working things out, claiming that all the experimenting didn't matter to him and he didn't want to lose me. So he promised we could work on a 'normal' sex life. Once again, as we all do, he was promising to sacrifice who he was in order to keep something he thought he wanted more.

He missed the point. A healthy sex life and a bit of kink are not necessarily mutually exclusive states; there should have been give and take. Ultimately, the problem was that H needed to experiment and he could not do this while in a relationship with me, because I was not fully willing. I am concerned not to perpetuate a common reaction of transvestites as perverts, as many couples experiment in their physical relationship and there is absolutely nothing wrong with that. But, whatever you like to do in the bedroom, a couple's sex life should be two-way. Mine and H's was very one sided and I was losing out. This was something H was not appreciating.

The lesson here is that, if your partner becomes disinterested in sex or you think that you might both want very different things from your sex life, talk about it fully, thoroughly and honestly. Be prepared to seek help outside of the relationship—preferably sooner rather than later. If you do not want the same things, it is better to make informed choices about where the relationship is going and not waste any more time if you are simply incompatible.

H was promising to try and 'fix' our sex life at this very late stage. He said he would seek help where he had refused to previously; he suggested couples counselling. I believe in working things out if you can and I believe in both partners pulling their weight when it comes to repairing the relationship. Maybe because it was so late in the day, this principle of mine momentarily went out the window when he suggested we both go and see someone about his lack of desire.

Frankly, I was indignant at this suggestion.

'I'm not going to see anyone, I am not the one who has a problem with physical affection,' I spat with involuntarily venom.

Please do not misunderstand me; I have every sympathy with men who experience problems in the bedroom department and in a manner of speaking, I was sympathetic to H, but he clearly had a deep problem with not wanting to be touched, and avoiding all physicality. I realised it went beyond any physiological problems there may have been—which I believe were literally due to it not being used. Hey, 'Use it or lose it', right? The problem was that he didn't want to use it.

H needed to work out what he wanted before promising anything to anyone he was to have a relationship with. I truly hope that he has done this and can now accept himself as trans—hopefully he is closer to understanding where on the spectrum he is, and is happier for it. In the end, I do not believe that he could achieve this at the same time as having to consider someone else's needs. At some point I recognised that I really wanted a traditional, tender, love-making sex life, and it became evident that I could not have with this with H.

Call me selfish or whatever you like, but I had reached the stage where I was not prepared to hang around while H tried to 'sort himself out' sexually and I was not going to wait and see if we could achieve the level of sex life I wanted. That was too big an 'if'. I'd already had enough (or more to the point, not nearly enough!) and I'd been starved for too long. Someone else had told me I was attractive, beautiful—sexy, even— and that my partner was insane for not seeing what was right in front of him. I was gaining confidence and realised I was in my sexual prime. I'd had very little sex in my life and this suddenly felt very, very wrong.

Much as an alternative, experimental sex life can be immensely satisfying, loving, pleasurable—and dare I say, healthy—in the case of submissive/dominant role play, it absolutely must be practised with love, not anger, resentment or hate. Safe and consensual sex is exactly that, however you choose to have it, and it includes you both having a healthy mental attitude towards it.

From the very beginning of our relationship, H made me feel that I wanted disproportionate amounts of sex, as though I was some kind of nymphomaniac. Hardly! I therefore should have seen that we were clearly incompatible and doomed from the outset. I think the issue was that at that stage, I had low self-esteem—just another of those things that affects you more when you are young. H had shown an interest in me and that was all it took to win me over. It was just that the 'I can't keep my hands off you!' stage was one-sided. I'm no sex fiend. This wasn't really about sex so much as it was about a fundamental lack of any physical comfort during the relationship. H didn't want comforting touches. Very occasionally, he would want to hug, and we did hold hands.

I know now that I am a tactile person and that I show care, compassion and comfort with physical touch. I show love and affection with hugs and kisses when I greet friends and family. Physical communication is a very powerful way of communicating all kinds of love. Yet, I didn't have this outlet with H. Even when his mother died— and then his father, a year later—he would not be comforted. He would insist that there was 'no point to it'. In addition, he made me feel like my words were useless, pointless, insignificant and unhelpful. His primary communication was that of spoken word. He was so eloquent and proficient in the use of words that my primary communication of body language felt stupid and clumsy by comparison. I felt constantly at fault for my perceived lack of effectiveness in comforting him. I am glad that I now know clearly how I express love and how I need it reciprocated.

So as you can tell, I have experienced the polar opposites of sexual relationships. As much as I do not advocate the use of 'right' and 'wrong', the two relationships I have described are, for me, exactly that; wrong and oh-so-very right. The difference is my perception, rather than the perception of the masses. Making love with Nicci is right for me and the way Nicci and I communicate physically has been noted by others in our lives. SJ described her view of the way the two of us interact.

'The two of you have your giggles and you have your flirts, but you have your physical side, which is more tender', she said, which I felt was put rather beautifully. 'I see the occasional touches when you pass each other; it's almost like the two of you can't go past one another without at least brushing against the other person and acknowledging them. Men don't generally do this—or it has to be crude, like a pinch on the arse and a comment. With you two it is very hidden, a very quiet touch.

'When you sit together, you don't necessarily touch, or you could be touching but it is not sexual touching,' SJ continued. 'You'll have your legs draped over Nicci, and she'll have her hand resting on your knee; it's a relaxed comforting thing that isn't passionate and isn't uncomfortable for people around you to see.

'I have seen you at social events, when it is clear you have spent the afternoon having sex—it's obvious; you are just so keyed into each other. You still have conversations with everyone and are still actively engaged with everyone but when you look at each other, it's like there is no-one else in the room! It's really nice to see. So, you have all the stuff that every woman wants; there is something else about you that is passionate, but not sexually. I have watched the two of you talk about things that you might discuss with a big group to get a debate going— you two have these discussions, and both respect that what the other is saying is worth listening to'.

People, particularly the British, have made sex a forbidden topic over the years. Mostly, in the past (but I am sure still today to some extent), sexual positions were restricted to missionary with the lights off. It was relegated as simply for procreation. Religions have dominated people's thoughts and behaviours on sex for centuries. There is no forbidden question as far as I am concerned, as it is an opportunity for me to educate, and if the question is too personal then I can choose not to answer it. However, sometimes the way that some people go about broaching this subject does amuse me; it marks the extent to which the human race has made the conversation of sex uncomfortable. I will give you an example.

We were at a large conference where Nicci had given a speech. During the break, a lovely gentleman approached Nicci to congratulate her on it, commenting on how moving he thought it was. He then shifted his weight awkwardly from one foot to the other, looked over each shoulder a few times, leant towards both of us and spoke to us in a low voice.

'Do you mind if I ask you both a personal question?' he asked.

We encouraged him to continue and he paused awkwardly again before speaking.

'How does it work?' he asked, cocking his head from me to Nicci. 'You know?'

Neither of us cottoned on immediately, so the man clarified for us.

'You know … downstairs?' At this point, I should add that Nicci was presenting as fully female that day.

'I am a fully functional biological male,' Nicci told the man, assuming that was the intelligent and most professional way of answering—particularly as this was a conference being held for educational establishments. However, it didn't seem to work; the man looked confused, bewildered even.

'But what about …?' he indicated at Nicci's cleavage, staring.

Nicci dropped the professional act and switched to her usual cheeky self.

'Darling,' she said, 'these are all scaffolding and padding—there's nothing real there.'

The man was taken aback but the penny dropped and it broke the ice.

What you do in the bedroom with your partner is private. However, even those on the transgendered scene and spectrum feel such confusion by how it works, it may require some exploration. It is the area that I am sure people make the most assumptions about. Whereas they might be brave enough to ask probing questions on other areas about how our relationship 'works' with Nicci being transgender, they are less likely to ask questions about our sex life.

The most common question I have personally been asked in

regards to the bedroom is a variation on: 'Do you see him as a her, or a him?' or 'Are you making love to a man or a woman?' Those pesky little labels and prescribed roles again! Do you remember the gender roles I talked about previously: 'He takes out the rubbish,' etc.? Well, equally I feel that there are expected gender roles in the bedroom. The expectations women may have of men in the bedroom are usually based on the bedrock that they are masculine in appearance—and certainly that they only wear men's clothes in everyday life.

There is a difference between trans and non-trans relationships. I say this from my experience, but I do not think it is unique, judging by conversations I have had with other women in trans relationships. The difference is that the trans woman does, to a varying degree, want to experience what it feels like to be feminine in the bedroom when making love with their partners. Ultimately, foreplay ends in penetrative sex—but foreplay for the man wearing women's underwear is as close as it gets to making love as a woman.

I am sure that people have a whole plethora of assumptions swimming around their heads about how it works. Some may be judgemental or wildly inaccurate. Some people may even feel disgusted. I genuinely do not care what people think of me, because it doesn't matter. They are not the ones who take my partner's hand and walk with her to the bedroom to show how much they love her. Only two people matter and I am not afraid to share with others how good our sex life is …. In the right context, of course. I don't go around shouting it from the rooftops, or bending the ear of anyone who will listen while ignoring their increasing looks of discomfort. I think that people are OK with Ann Summers-type experimenting in the bedroom between couples, but many find anything more adventurous a bit uncomfortable to hear about.

When asked about people's expectations of her and her partner's sexual relationship, one trans partner I interviewed put it rather succinctly.

'Straight, bi, gay, trans; we all have things we like, things we love and things we dislike', she said. 'Whatever you like, it's about being able to communicate it to your partner', she finished, to my mind hitting the nail on the head.

Within a loving relationship, sex can be the most beautiful and powerful expression of your love you can give. You literally cannot be physically closer with someone than you are when you are making love. Since the beginning of mankind, it has been one of the most natural acts in the world. In these difficult financial times, it really is the most fun you can have for free (and I do mean free; birth control pills in the UK are available on the NHS at no cost). Sex is life giving—and I don't mean just in the context of procreation. The energy and power of giving yourself and another human being such pleasure is immeasurable. Why do we deny ourselves, why do we make the most natural and beautiful act between two people unnecessarily uncomfortable?

Nicci and I did not flee from our respective relationships and run into one another's arms. We both gave ourselves time and space … until we couldn't wait any longer! I believe sex is in our hearts and minds. In a relationship, it is an expression of the strength of feeling you have for one another. There is anticipation and an electricity of expectation and excitement. During many of the discussions Nicci and I had as friends, we both had the revelation that sharing affection was part of many of the aspects which we agreed were most important to us.

What was undoubtedly excitement about having sex with Nicci for the first time had also become a need. I suppose there was an element of nervousness but I don't remember it. I knew without doubt that the sex would be good … but, oh, my, God! I did not expect it to be so absolutely amazing—easily the most powerful orgasm I'd had in my whole life. It was honest, real, raw sexual animalism.

That wasn't all of it, though. At that point, we had become so close in mind, intellect and friendship that it was the ultimate act in physical expression. I was 32 years old and, for the very first time, sex was beautiful and moving. It still is today.

The Pitfalls

I wouldn't be a normal person if I had not at first worried, had doubts and fears about my relationship with Nicci—but my worries were not because of who she was, but rather because of my anticipation of the future and what it might hold in terms of the reactions of society and my family. The situations this brought up was something I was inevitably going to have to tackle.

Once, we went to SJ's birthday party at her house, and just like any other couple, we got chatting to people over the course of the night. We hit it off really well with one particular couple, and Nicci ended up talking to the wife in the kitchen; I to the husband in the garden. Throughout all this, Nicci's being transgender was never once mentioned—we talked about the ordinary stuff of daily life: jobs, the family, and football matches on Saturday.

However, I later heard feedback from SJ that when we walked into the party, the wife of this couple had asked: 'What is that?' Now, having got to know this couple throughout the evening, I found this hilarious; I could imagine it was exactly the sort of thing she would say. It also illustrates that our friends are comfortable being honest with both Nicci and I when talking about trans issues. No doubt SJ knew I would find it funny.

Quite apart from anything else, it occurs to me that people's judgments vary too much from person to person. The best example I can think of concerns the young girl I wrote about earlier, Debbie, who showed such fascination on the subject of my and Nicci's sexuality. After clearing that issue up, we had an even more interesting conversation at the bar later that evening.

'I think you are amazing!' she exclaimed. I asked her why she thought this.

'I wouldn't tolerate a partner who put a dress on,' she explained. 'I'd be out the door, or throwing him out. But you are in public with your partner in a dress—and you appear to be a very happy couple. You come across as a woman who is very happy in your relationship. I would be mortified and worried about what everyone else in the place was thinking of me.'

We talked about the fact that I had found someone I was comfortable with and discussed how I wasn't willing to let anyone else's judgements stop me living the life I had chosen—however admittedly out of the ordinary it was. As the conversation progressed, she went on to tell me that the boyfriend she was with that night had, in fact, only been seeing her for a few weeks; she intended to drown her sorrows that night, because her previous fiancé had left her a few months ago for another woman who was having his baby. The woman in question was seven months pregnant when Debbie's fiancé left, and that was two months prior to this meeting; so, as it happened, the other woman's baby was due that very day.

Now, please do not misunderstand me—I am not judging anyone else's life and am certainly in no position to throw stones—but I do wonder how women can endure a relationship so full of betrayal and yet, if their partner ever 'put on a dress', these women claim that they would be 'out the door'. I have a partner who loves and adores me, protects me and cherishes me—and, I believe, is highly unlikely to ever cheat on me. Despite all this, some other women genuinely think I must be mad for choosing to be with her. Whereas I could easily shrug off looks and stares in public (though I rarely notice them), I can't imagine how long might it take your average person to get over the greater humiliation of Debbie's ordeal. I cannot be 'mortified' about Nicci's choice of clothes; I get to go home happily with my partner.

Regardless, I was touched that—though Debbie confessed that my and Nicci's relationship was against her beliefs—she did also say that if she had been so very uncomfortable with how Nicci was dressed, she and her boyfriend would have left the pub—and told everyone why they were leaving. I was thankful to her for staying that night but I would have been just as respectful if she had felt strongly enough to leave; other people might have expected Nicci and me to leave instead. The difference was that this woman, who I only ever met the one time, was honest enough with herself to realise that her discomfort would be entirely her own problem, therefore she should be the one to leave. I respected her honesty that night, and her lack of any sign of ashamedness when asking questions—she was genuinely trying to understand.

The main thing is that all of us should hold our heads high in public and be honest about who we are. Nicci started on this path of self-honesty in her late 30s and I in my early 30s—not to mention my grandma, for whom I will always have fond memories (particularly in her later years); she had a boyfriend as late as her 80s. She went on holidays with him, her sitting around the pool in her bikini, living everyday of her life as if it was to be her last, always looking forward to the next party, having the best possible time even on her deathbed. She simply refused to be what people expected of a woman in her 80s. I say to you, it is never too late to start living, so start now! I will even forgive you if you put down this book.

৪০৫৪

Are you still with me? Well that's OK. I really would like you to enjoy my story to the end and actually, it might be good if you have some idea what you could be up against while living life as a rebel.

Once you start on a certain path, the excitement and thrill of freedom can be exhilarating. You'll feel as though nothing can touch you—you are beyond reproach, safe up in your bubble. Eventually the helium will start to leak out and you will gently drift back down to earth, only just beginning to notice that others are looking at you as though you are a loon. They might not realise how suffocating their daily existence is and that it could be much lighter if they just allow themselves to let go. They may not know how to let go.

Now I am at risk of sounding like a hippie, I should say that, all joking aside, the freedom I have found has been a rollercoaster ride. When you decide to take risks and change something in your life, you need to keep some wits about you; a level-headedness about exactly how far you want to take things. Being in a trans relationship can be tough at times and love is sometimes not enough; in some relationships, the negatives can outweigh that love or overpower it in time. Being in a relationship with someone who is trans may very well mean that a woman may have to compromise in so many areas.

It can be very easy for the woman of a trans partner to put herself second. As solid as we are, I will take an example of Nicci and me: we were both getting ready for a party and were both having one of those times when you are not sure what to wear. I had changed a few times, as each thing I put on just didn't feel right. Nicci was in the same frame of mind.

This was fairly early on in our relationship and I felt a little awkward about being so indecisive when I felt I didn't have the 'right' to be—to my mind, it was more important for Nicci to be comfortable. Tensions were running high at this point and just before we left the flat, Nicci asked me again what I thought about her final chosen outfit. I said she looked good, but when she went to the bedroom to take another final look, she was angry.

'I look like a tranny!' she exclaimed.

I interpreted her statement to be accusatory, as if she was asking me how I could let her go out looking like that. I was hurt but the censorship rule came to the rescue once again, as I said she had made me feel my opinion was invalid. I have as much right as Nicci to have an off-night and be unsure of myself and, frankly, to have a wobbly moment as she does.

It is a demonstration of the beauty of the no censorship rule that we have never had the same disagreement again.

I have gained and developed a better view since then of what suits her because, over time, I have seen her try a wider variety of outfits. On top of this, talked about the issue, dealt with our feelings and moved on, not allowing it to fester and grow into more than it was. It is irrelevant that the issue was about something related to Nicci being transgendered, because all issues can and should be dealt with in this way in all relationships.

In a trans relationship, where your partner is 'out', I think the root of situations such as the above comes from a feeling of protective nurturing. As a woman in a trans relationship, you are aware that there is a certain element of vulnerability to your partner. The motivation behind my thinking that it was more important for Nicci to look and feel good, was that I was not going to risk having her potentially stared at by strangers. Looking as naturally womanly as possible and not a 'drag act', is important for trans women.

At the very beginning of our relationship, Nicci was unconvinced that I was truly as willing to accept all aspects of her being transgender, as I claimed—no matter how much I insisted on my supportiveness. It was only once our relationship started to unfold and develop over time, with concrete examples, that she began to understand that I genuinely believe that she has the right to be herself and that I have no right to place any limits, parameters, rules or caveats on the trans aspect of her (or indeed any other aspect).

Although obviously in all relationships there may be something about the other person that you are not one hundred per cent happy with, if you love someone you have to accept them for themselves and not expect them to change, nor ask for it. I embrace the aspects of Nicci which make her a woman in my mind. When she is presenting or even displaying an aspect of herself that is feminine, she is a woman as far as I am concerned.

However, many partners of trans girls are frightened of bucking the trends of what is acceptable by society, and so will place restrictions on how, when and where they 'allow' their partner to express their transgender nature. If we suggested that we were 'allowing' any other person to express a part of their personality, the person would—quite rightly—be outraged. Yet women on the trans scene do seem to set limitations. Sometimes, the condition is that (s)he doesn't 'dress' in the company of a certain friend, or member of the family. Each time I think I have found another woman like me, in my situation, who is as like-minded about the subject, I uncover some element that gives Nicci the opportunity to remind me that I am remarkable and unique. I wish this weren't the case. I am hopeful that there are more women out there who, like me, are as fully accepting of their partner's transgender nature, and I have simply not met them yet.

The pattern in many trans relationships is that the trans partner is so grateful that their wife, girlfriend, partner is willing to accept their more 'unusual' characteristic, they will accept any rules that make their partner more comfortable with 'allowing' their transgender personality to exist. In short, they take what they can get. For the trans person, it is such a difficult confession to make to a loved one. They do not want to squander or undermine the confidence and trust they have built with that person. You could argue the relationship is more highly prized than other relationships, because it is rare.

Therefore, from the trans perspective, they are more likely to stay in the relationship and stay monogamous, regardless of its restrictions. Starting each new relationship brings with it the trauma of confessing all over again. Unfortunately, this means that trans people may not be able to see that they are not in such a healthy relationship; if their wife, girlfriend or partner is asking them to restrict part of who they are, it is because they feel discomfort. Rather than deal with this discomfort, they would rather their partner simply stop temporarily—without realising this is not so simple.

In addition to worries within the relationship, there are a lot of intense physical and emotional changes for the trans person to cope with outside of it. Sometimes, they have transitioned while on the roller-coaster, so end up having a horrific realisation once they have had gender reassignment surgery, panicking and feeling that it was a drastic mistake. This is an extremely uncommon example that often is overridden after the initial shock has worn off, but once again those evil little boxes rear their persistent heads from the shadows and people are simply swept off into just joining another category, rather than challenging the fact that one size does not fit all. Since Nicci currently has no intention of going down that route, that particular worry is on the sidelines.

'Your acceptance of her being transgender has made Nicci question what she really wants,' SJ said, the implication being that Nicci does not feel the need to go the whole way—she can simply be herself. Not all people on the transgendered spectrum feel as though they have that choice—some feel like they must pick one side of a duality. SJ even considered that Nicci could have gone down the path of 'seriously thinking about becoming homosexual.' Changed sexual preference is something that some male-to-female trans women consider—or discover.

Far worse, some transgendered people get so much stick for their pure and genuine wish to embrace their true gender, they suffer horrible treatment from their acquaintances and can become depressed. I know of a case where a transgendered person, a regular visitor to A&E, has made repeated attempts to commit suicide. The staff members have come to know him well and (off the record) he has told them that his neighbours are harassing him on a daily basis, with vicious attacks on him physically and verbally and damaging his property. He has said that they have been doing so for some time. His fear is so extensive that he does not want the reason for his attempted suicides documented in his medical notes, as he does not wish Social Services, police or any other officials to be made aware of the situation, for fear of the repercussions.

As horrible as this situation is, it is all too easy when you are new to the trans scene to come to expect adversity, regardless of whether or not it is there. Once, Nicci called me unexpectedly at work and said a friend had offered us tickets to go to an A-Ha concert that night with his partner at the last minute. I jumped at the chance. It hit home that going out into the big wide world was different to the trans clubs, because Nicci's vulnerability was obvious on the packed train on the way home. Her visible desperation to place herself in a position where she could least be stared at literally made my heart ache. It was the first, but not the last time I had that overwhelming protective instinct. I wanted to put my arms around her and make her safe. I wanted to fight for her and challenge those passengers around us who were staring. I was indignant. 'How dare they stare at her!' I thought to myself.

I have relaxed a little and become more accustomed to people looking in public. I have realised that it is her fight, not mine; she has to face whatever demons arise and I can only stand on the sidelines and trust that I will know when to step in—and that she would ask for support if she needed it. She has to manage situations herself and is more than capable of doing so. I wondered that day how I would react the first time she did have a negative reaction in public, as it seemed inevitable. This event was now years ago and we have still never had one outright negative reaction we have had to deal with. People still do stare and always will. I don't like it and of course Nicci hates it, but I am mellowing. People are curious, it is human nature.

Things are changing, slowly, in a positive direction and we can only ask for things to continue on that course. Attitudes will not transform overnight any more than a transsexual's gender issues will be solved overnight. I don't know whether the issue is becoming more accepted or if people genuinely just have an indifferent attitude and don't react as I initially expect them to; either way, very quickly into my and Nicci's relationship, I stopped waiting to have to deal with a bad reaction from people, because I have never directly been on the receiving end of one.

I know better, now, than to take offense at every little thing. I can no longer care less what the average 'man on the street' (for want of a better phrase) thinks of me, my partner and our relationship. I will happily answer their questions, if they want to learn. As for my friends and family, I should not have had any fears on that score; I'm not saying it was all plain sailing, but people have been surprisingly unfazed by it all, and those closest to me are pleased to see how happy the relationship makes me, and that is all that really matters.

A Class Act

I f you were to ask my definition of Nicci, I would say that she is a normal thinking and feeling woman and dresses as such; in a stylish, classic and feminine way. She does not walk down the street looking like a parody or pastiche of woman, causing discomfort everywhere she goes. When I say 'walk down the street', I am not speaking figuratively; she does walk down the street dressed as a woman. She goes shopping, to restaurants, to the theatre and all the rest of it dressed as a woman.

Nicci suits both genders and her identity is neither fully male nor female. She is comfortable with both sides of herself and expresses this with her outward appearance. I recognise that Nicci is transgendered (not transsexual) and has a male side, so therefore is able to behave as the man in the relationship; to lavish physical attention on me, as the woman, in an amount I am more than satisfied with.

Overall, however, she would prefer to be thought of in the feminine.

I am happy enough about Nicci's gender identity. As an individual, she is someone I love, so whether or not she is he or she does not seem all that relevant. I always call her Nicci, though I know I am fairly unique in this respect; in my experience other partners of trans people use separate male or female names for their partner depending on how they are dressed. There is probably a multitude of different methods partners use; I have a friend who is similar to me, in so as much as she mostly refers to her partner as Sarah even when referring to Sarah as 'him' to friends and family. She finds this confuses them, (as you might expect) and they struggle with how easily she can swap between her usage of different genders.

'You treat transgender as if it is the most natural thing in the world,' our friend SJ said to me. 'Yes, Nicci's friends had accepted it all, but that is not the same as your partner accepting it.'

It is interesting quite how many people say that I treat the subject of being in a relationship with a trans woman as 'the most natural thing in the world' (always in those exact words). I can't help but wonder if they have subliminally read me and identified that I live my life in a way that is natural to me. Moreover, I think it draws Nicci to me as much as I am drawn to her.

I feel uncomfortable taking any credit for Nicci's development as a woman. Yes, she might have done more because I have encouraged her, and our friends indicate that my attitude towards everything has helped enormously, but I don't think that it is anything she would not have achieved on her own over a longer period of time. With the support of her friends, she would get there eventually; it will always take time, as after all, Nicci missed out of the experience of growing up as a female.

As a result, she also missed out on the experience of being a little girl. From my point of view, it seems right to make up for it in adulthood. Don't panic—I am not about to launch into describing some kinky side of my and Nicci's relationship! Baby play is fine if you are into that sort of thing (as some people are) but it is definitely not for me. I am talking about the little things, like being called Princess by an adult in your life or someone close to you.

Many of us in relationships, have pet names for our partners; one day, when Nicci was feeling ill and I was at work, I called her to give her some love and sympathy and said to her (for no particular reason); 'I'm sorry you are feeling rough, my Princess.' It came naturally to me and as such, the name stuck. I don't actually call her Princess that often, so when I do it makes it more special.

As for how others respond to Nicci, there have been mixed

responses. Nicci understands that others may struggle with who she is and so tries to help people feel comfortable in her company. She encourages, in turn helping them to understand. Nicci never judges when people do not understand; she is patient and will take the time to really discuss all the issues they may be struggling with. I guess that is the teacher in her. My family have been wonderful about the whole thing, but it would be wrong to suggest that my dad, at least, did not have some reservations about meeting Nicci in full feminine splendour.

The first year Nicci and I were together, I invited my family to my new flat for Christmas dinner. My dad was an hour late and I knew that he was really very uncomfortable about facing the prospect of seeing Nicci dressed as a woman. His view was—and I think, still is—another one of the classic preconceptions that 'dressing up as a girl' is something Nicci does, not who she is. As a result, I suppose Dad wondered why she had to do it in front of him, thinking it was the sort of thing that should remain behind closed doors.

Fair play to him; Dad did turn up—and, to the relief of both my parents, Nicci was not wearing a dress. She wore jeans, a blouse and subtle make-up. I am sure they thought they were going to meet the Nicci version of Danny La Rue.

'You don't have to worry about that with Nicci,' SJ said. 'Everything she wears is subtle. She is very classy and I think that it is why I am comfortable being in her company—because she is not over the top.'

It wasn't always this way. Initially, Nicci had to find her feet. I didn't know her at this stage, so I was fascinated when interviewing her friends about what she was like at the beginning.

'When I first met her, she wasn't as confident,' mused SJ. 'Every time she did dress, she dressed the whole way; make-up, eye lashes, hair, clothes. Everything was so co-ordinated, everything was stunning.'

Another friend described her view of Nicci's tentative steps at coming out in a supportive environment.

'Nicci is confident now, but it hasn't always been that way,' this friend said. 'She must have been this big-time rugby macho boy on the outside to all her friends, trying to keep this secret—trying to keep up appearances but desperately wanting to tell people the truth. What's telling is that she told all the girls she was closest to first; those who wouldn't judge her. Next were some of the quieter guys who wouldn't blab. She chose the people she could trust; the gentler people—like she was dipping her toe in the water.'

This is obvious really, but imagine the strength and courage this took; not knowing how people would react or if she would lose loved ones. Nicci is one of the lucky ones—everyone close to her has accepted her as transgender. She can still be the huge rugby fan that she is, but is embraced by the girls on a girl's night out too.

Annie's observations were very enlightening. She described what I imagine was possibly the 'study' stage of Nicci's learning to be feminine. I asked Annie if she thought there was a difference between Nicci presenting as female as opposed to male.

'Only a slight one now, but there was a big difference at first,' Annie explained. 'When she first visited us, say for a girls night in, she would look at how we behaved, how we sat, how we held ourselves—crossed our legs, everything—and try to copy. I was very conscious of it. Now she is totally relaxed and so am I. She doesn't watch us to learn anymore and I can tell the difference.

'Back then, I didn't like it when Nicci dressed up.' Annie confessed. 'She would sit up properly—uptight—too much like a proper lady.'

We had a fit of the giggles at the idea of Nicci being more of a 'lady' than us. Annie said that it made her feel uncomfortable; she felt she wasn't holding herself or behaving in a ladylike enough way, so it became a weird turn of the tables when she then found herself studying Nicci on how to be a 'lady'!

Annie's description was hilarious:

'You never knew if you were going to have the 'uptight lady' turn up! It was a relief when the guy showed up instead—just because I didn't have to think of my own behaviour,' she said. 'Now she has learnt how to be a woman and I am much more relaxed in her company and happier.'

We're back to that awkward teenage girl again: 'She was just going through a phase!'

SJ once observed that, where Nicci has had to reinvent herself, she has found so much more to talk about, and is no longer embarrassed to talk about anything, whether it be from the point of view of a guy or a girl.

'I've seen him be very contented, but she is different', she said. 'But then, we all are when we have spent time getting dressed up for a night out, because as women, we care what people think and we want to look nice—even for other women. These days, she is just as comfortable talking about rugby as she is about the challenges of sticking on false eye lashes.'

Others have noticed this. One friend noted that she was happier listening to Nicci talk and engaging in conversation than she was with other guys and that talking to both of us is so easy—the effect of us being so comfortable with one another makes others in our company feel comfortable. I thought that was a beautiful thing to say about a couple's relationship. Dare I say that the compliment made me blush!

As so many other trans women, Nicci has not always been an expert on what it is to be a woman. Her close friends have seen her transformation perhaps to a greater extent than me. This could be because she had been out for two years when I met her—or simply because she is my partner and the subtle changes that happen over time pass over you when you are with someone day in, day out. For friends who see her less may notice that on each occasion has developed more.

'Her confidence has grown in leaps and bounds,' she commented. 'It's like gay guys; nine times out of ten they have better taste in clothes than women. There is something about Nicci—she knows exactly what she likes. Everything is done to her taste and with confidence. But I think that has something to do with her relationship with you—you have given her the space and the input she may not have received from others. Whereas they might be afraid to say anything, you might say; "I like you in this, but that would suit you more." You have given her the freedom to just be. So, I think she has come a long way since she has been with you.'

Both SJ and Annie described how Nicci now looks so much more relaxed in her own skin—that she will wear comfier, everyday clothes and her hair will look nice. They added that she might have less make-up on, but her nails on some days will be painted and perfect. She has settled into just being.

Nicci is very confident, but sometimes—particularly more so in the early years of our relationship—there was a tension before we walked out the door for a night out. I sometimes forget that she spent 40 years of her life practicing hiding her true feeling to a level of expertise. I have seen this diminish more and more during the time I have been with her; I have seen her walk out the door some days as a confident beautiful woman. But this is the same for all of us—we are not all confident women every day. That's life.

Getting to a point where Nicci didn't feel pressurised into embracing one part of herself over the other has been quite a journey. I wasn't with her from the beginning, but one distinctive memory comes to mind from that first year we were together. Like all of us, she had a moment of feeling the need to put herself in the little boxes that are expected of us. We were about to get ready to go out to meet a trans couple we knew in a trans-friendly pub for a karaoke night. Nicci was prevaricating when getting ready.

'I can't be bothered to shave and put make-up on,' she said. 'But I should, shouldn't I?'

'Why should you?' I asked—something I thought to be a perfectly reasonable question.

I can't remember her answer, but I remember it was something to do with the fact that we were going somewhere trans friendly. I reminded her that she was 'out' now, which meant that she did not have to grab every opportunity to dress in a feminine way. She was going somewhere where it was accepted; she could go anywhere at any time dressed as a woman, whenever she wanted to. I stress when she wanted, not when she felt she that should. I reminded her that all the bravery and adversity she had overcome was so she could have the freedom of choice—that means no 'should', no expectation; pure unadulterated choice and it would be her choice, not mine or anyone else's. When we arrived at the bar that night, Nicci was unshaved, wearing a T-shirt, jeans and boots. Our friends did look a little taken aback but Nicci was totally unapologetic and just said she didn't feel like being a girl that night.

Who Am I, if He Becomes She?

I t is not out of the realms of possibility that Nicci may one day want to transition fully. At this point in time, it seems very unlikely— but we must never say 'never'. Consider that previously, I painted two very different pictures of sex lives that I have experienced. If I were to have to go back to a relationship where penetrative sex was non-existent (and had to justify that 'other' activities constituted as a sex life), I can't imagine I would ever be happy with that sex life again. The next big question is what would happen if (and it is a big 'if') my partner was to decide that she wanted to fully transition to being a woman.

'So, how will you deal with it if Nicci decides to transition the whole way?'

People have often asked. I give my usual answer, to the tune of 'life is too short for "what ifs" and I'm happy right now and I deal with one day at a time.' I know that there could be problems, as illustrated by another trans partner I spoke to on the subject.

'There was pressure on both of us,' she told me. 'I felt it particularly when she was trying to decide what to do about transitioning. I wanted desperately to support her while she was having such a hard time but was also dealing with the reality that, every time I was supportive of her, I was also pushing her one step further away from me.

'I knew that, ultimately, we could not stay together if she transitioned. My partner knew this too and would then become more worried about talking to me for fear of making me feel worse—which in turn would upset me, because she wasn't talking to me.'

You can see how not dealing with things, however painful, can make matters more complicated.

'This situation created a vicious circle,' this woman continued. 'We were both scared to say what we were thinking for fear of upsetting the other.'

There's that all important word again: 'fear'. It grips every single one of us as human beings at some time in our lives, if not many times. I have friends who, as much as they love Nicci deep down, are concerned about how the relationship could affect me in the future, should she decide to transition. My family also have their concerns. I remember the first and only in-depth conversation I had with my dad about Nicci being transgendered.

'What happens when he wants to start taking hormones and have an operation?' he asked me.

This is a fair question and he was not the only one to have raised it. I think he was genuinely bemused why I would want to be in such a relationship, but then again, I was equally bemused to find that my father knew about such things as 'hormones' and 'the op'! So there you go—he caught me off guard as well. After that, I went off on my scripted description of the gender spectrum again. You aren't the first one to be on the receiving end of that spiel!

'Nicci could have gone down the road of taking hormones,' SJ said, later clarifying that if going the whole way with transition was what Nicci genuinely wanted, then there was absolutely nothing wrong with that. She reasoned that it was not essential because Nicci had found me; meeting me had given Nicci the opportunity to feel what it was like to be fully supported in just being herself. I will say that Nicci is far more comfortable with her transgender nature than most other trans women I know (indeed, this is a striking difference between her and H). Her level of confidence is attractive and liberating; it gives a deliciously infectious sense of freedom.

When I discussed it with a friend of mine, I was adamant that I was happy with how things were in my and Nicci's relationship. Even so, this friend still suggested that perhaps I should see a counsellor. I said that there was nothing to discuss with a counsellor, as I was happy with the relationship how it was. Her response was that it is good to talk regardless—she asked if I would at least consider it if it seemed that Nicci transitioning appeared to be on the horizon.

I don't expect any woman who has not been in a trans relationship to understand, but in my case even women who are in a trans relationship may not understand how I am so comfortable and supportive of the situation. I baffle people.

Ultimately, if Nicci thinks she may wish to transition, like all other things in our relationship, we will talk about it openly and honestly—however raw, hurtful and difficult it may become. We have promised to always have no censorship, ever. For some women, sadly any such kind of decision may be taken out of their hands; if their partner decides to transition, for them this may mean a change in which gender they are choosing to have a sexual relationship with.

To me, nothing matters more than being true to myself, irrespective of the specifics of the situation. If I feel that staying in the relationship is compromising to my sense of self and there is no workable solution, then I may have to consider the unthinkable; walking away. As painful and devastating as this may be, it is true of all relationships, not just trans partners. The key is that, if you have not lost yourself in the relationship, you do have the strength to deal with anything. Just believe.

So: the question of who I am if he becomes she. In this context, it is only relevant to me if I am concerned about society wishing to categorise my sexuality, which I am not. Yes, I think it is an interesting debate, though I don't have the answer; for me it is irrelevant, because who I am as a person is not dependant on whether or not Nicci will transition.

Essentially, the pleasure and intimacy we get from sex is a very important part of our relationship and neither of us wants to lose this.

'Nicci as a man, is very manly,' Carol observed. 'I've asked if she would go as far as complete gender change; she has said that she would not, because she is with you and the physical relationship between you two is at the point where Nicci will never do anything to disrupt that.'

I think I could handle most of the physiological changes that come with transition, if they were something Nicci wanted. One thing I am certain about however, is that irrespective of its sexual category, I want to be in a relationship with someone who has a penis. As much as this sounds crude, I am boiling it down to biological basics. I have had this conversation with Nicci, explaining that I do not want her to lose her male appendage—the last fundamental biological aspect making her male.

Not that any of the other changes would necessarily be easy to deal with—there is a possibility that they would prove too much for me to handle. For example, there is the issue of hormones. The introduction of the female hormone, oestrogen, into a male body may affect Nicci's ability for male sexual function—it may be almost equal to her actually losing her penis, as they would most likely render her unable to use it for making love. That said, Mother Nature is a powerful thing and Nicci knows a couple where the husband started his transition (i.e. started to take the hormones) and he and his wife were still able to have sex. Not only that, but her wife became pregnant!

I realise at this point that the topic of motherhood is something I have yet to broach. I agree that hormones would leave me in a rather a tricky predicament, if I did want children; but have no fear—we can leave this topic there, as I do not. Nicci and I have no desire to start a family, so this is not part of the equation. I realise we are in a good situation in this regard, as I am sure children do complicate a trans relationship and I acknowledge this for those who are in that situation.

Interestingly, Nicci is at the stage where she says that she is happier with being male that she has ever been in her life. To me, this is evidence of my theory that in a relationship, you must be able to be totally free to be yourself, including embracing all aspects of your gender identity, if that is relevant to you. I believe that Nicci feels comfortable because she has had the time, space and freedom to fully explore her female side, uninhibited.

This means that, instead of resenting her male side because she has been 'forbidden' to express her female side, she has been able to explore how she feels about both and arrive at a place where she is happy and comfortable being male and female. She loves her Russell and Bromley brogues as much as her New Look dresses.

'She feels comfortable in his relationship with you, she likes to dress and doesn't see herself wanting "the chop"', a friend of ours sums up succinctly.

The whole issue does beg the question; would I be back to square one if Nicci transitioned? By which I mean, it might be the same as when I was with H, i.e. no traditional sex life. There would be a difference this time around, in that I would be with the person I fell madly, deeply and passionately in love with. I feel loved and I love in return in a way that I have never known before. I have realised I need to express my love in a physical way, which is now reciprocated. So, if Nicci were to transition, it wouldn't be inconceivable that we could still express the same level of love, in a different way.

By and large, I feel that, in regards to transition, the question of 'Will she, won't she?' is almost redundant. Much as this is a more extreme example, the simple fact of the matter is that no one can say that, over the duration of their relationship, they definitely won't change. No one can guarantee that the passing years will show them to be the same person as at the beginning of the relationship; we are all entitled to change our opinions, aspects of our personality and adapt our thoughts according to our experiences.

I don't know how I will cope if Nicci changes but honestly, I very rarely think about it; I don't want to miss out on enjoying the present and all the positive aspects of being in a relationship by constantly over-analysing what would happen if things were to change.

Understanding, Acceptance, Integration

My experience of coming out (as being in a relationship with someone transgender) to everyone was that, in all my relationships, there was a marked improvement. I think it has also given me confidence. Everyone I have ever told is fascinated by my story, has plenty of questions and usually tells me I am brave, or how broadminded I am, or else how I must live an interesting life. Over time, I think this has made me stronger. I am not saying that I agree that I am 'brave' as such, but being unafraid to stand out in a crowd does seem to have made me a stronger person.

I am less afraid to say what I believe. I do not think I could have truthfully said this in the past. After I had told all my immediate family (having been with Nicci for a quite a while), we had the best ever meal out as a family that I can remember. Everyone was relaxed and genuinely enjoying each other's company. It will always be a good memory.

When I arranged a 65th birthday party for my mum, the atmosphere was the same. Nicci was not dressed femininely at either of these occasions but what the rest of the family saw was a happier me, a happier me than they had ever seen before; people have told me that how Nicci and I are together rubs off on those around us. On one occasion, a university friend and I looked at some old photos of us from years back.

'You look younger now than you did then,' she said, looking at me. 'You glow because you look happy. You are carefree.'

I am forever drawn into acknowledging how extremely lucky I am to have my family's understanding in regards to me and Nicci—well, if not 'understanding' as such, then at least 'accepting'; they are comfortable with it to varying degrees and have made it clear in many different ways that they accept Nicci as my partner and that we are happy together—and that is all that counts.

All those I have spoken to have highlighted that how well someone will accept trans people has much to do with their background—the social rules and politics they were they taught. One thing my dad told me when I was growing up (and I am absolutely sure he is not alone in this lesson) was: 'This is my house. When you grow up and you have your own house, you can do what you like in it.' There was some humour between us in me reminding him of this rule; I did not give it to him as an ultimatum or a threat, I simply told him that he was welcome in my home, that I wanted him to visit me—but he had to understand that, as it is my home, I was never going to ask Nicci to change.

These days, Dad does occasionally drop by unexpectedly and he must know that there could be a chance that Nicci is dressed in the feminine. I remember one late Sunday evening, he did exactly this. Nicci and I were in pyjamas—Nicci's were pink with dancing reindeer on them—and she was on the sofa with her feet up on the foot stool with dark painted toe nails. Dad is very observant and I can't believe it went unnoticed but credit where credit's due; he sat down, seemingly very relaxed in our company, and watched TV with us. My dad will not do anything that he doesn't want to—not for anyone, nor with any persuasion—so the fact that he has made an effort when I know he is not comfortable means a lot to me.

'I don't think that your relationship is conventional, but it obviously works for both of you,' my mum said to me one day, nearly two years into my and Nicci's relationship. 'You are happy and that is all that matters.'

The first time it really hit home for me that I was in a good position (as a partner of someone transgendered) was at the New Years' Eve party Nicci and I went to the first year we were together. It was at a friend's house and the host said not as many people as she hoped were going to be there—her parents included—because some of them could not be in the same room as her trans partner, dressed as female. That Christmas was the first time my parents had met Nicci dressed and although my dad was not comfortable, I realised that New Years Eve just how privileged I was to have my parents at my side—and how proud I was of them for not even kicking up a fuss. My dad had expressed a few disgruntled comments and was late on the day, but he turned up and sat and had Christmas dinner with Nicci wearing make-up, nevertheless.

The relationship this friend and her partner experienced had its rocky patches and she shared some of her concerns with me.

'I find it particularly difficult when my family refuse to see my partner "dressed",' she said. 'I mean, in female dress—not that they prefer to see him naked!' she added hastily, to our mutual amusement. 'I understand and respect their wishes, but it makes my life difficult when my parents refuse to be around my partner.'

Our friend has the same rule as me; if any of her friends and family members was to drop by to visit and her partner was dressed female, she would not even consider asking for her to change into male clothing. Whilst I have been lucky in that my friends and family have accepted this rule and have not been deterred from visiting us, sadly this friend found that visits dwindled and became non-existent. Her family simply did not want to be forced to face the issue.

However, when this friend explained the situation to her 80-year-old grandmother and showed her photos of her partner, the more mature and more forgiving elderly lady said she thought that our friends' partner made a lovely girl. I am convinced that my grandmother, who died at 88 without ever knowing about Nicci, would have had similar thinking. In fact, I am certain she would have absolutely loved Nicci; she was a woman who spent very little of her life sleeping because she said she didn't want to miss out on anything. Well into her 80s, she would sit up late and watch *Eurotrash*, laughing about the things people got up to. Maybe it's something about losing your inhibitions when you are older but I think we could all learn a lot from these two grannies.

This friend's partner told her she was beginning to think that she was transsexual and was considering becoming female full-time. My friend considered that the relationship might have to end, not because she did not love and accept her partner as being transsexual, but because it would break her heart to think of not being able to take her partner to family occasions such as birthdays.

Whilst my mum in particular has been fantastic about Nicci being transgender, I can understand that when it is your own child, it is a very different and more difficult to come to terms with. I will not go into details about how Nicci's family have dealt with her being trans as it is not my position to do so.

I will say that Nicci came out to her brother later rather than sooner, out of consideration for his two children (her nieces). Once the girls did know, we took one of Nicci's nieces shopping in Camden for a dress for her party for her 16th birthday and later we went on to Soho for something to eat. She was a little freaked out by 'being around so many gay people', as she put it.

'Darling, if you are freaked out by gay people, when you are older we will take you to a night out at a trans club—then you'll know what freaked out is!' Nicci replied, tongue-in-cheek.

I love Nicci's nieces to bits and her reply was classic.

'Oh, I won't be freaked out by that. That's just you in a dress with your other trans friends', she said.

Who can fully understand the mind of anyone, let alone that of a 16 year old? Nevertheless, we did talk seriously about things that day, not necessarily specific to trans issues but specific to not being afraid to be yourself. Nicci told her niece never to be afraid of being who she is and never to be apologetic for being herself. I hope she took it heart.

Nicci has amazing friends. Not everyone has found it easy but I think it is the unapologetic way that Nicci faces the world and shows her openness that attracts people to her; it is certainly what attracted me to her. Her close friends have accepted me into their homes, lives and hearts just as unquestioningly as they have Nicci. They have been incredibly accepting of Nicci and even fundamental to supporting her coming out—long before I ever knew her, though they essentially do not understand the concept of transgender. It is heart-warming they accept her regardless—I guess this is what friends should be like.

'I made no judgement on you wanting to be with a trans person,' Monica said when I first started seeing Nicci. 'I was just protective that you weren't going to hurt my friend. I liked that you knew all about it from the beginning because Nicci was upfront. She has boxed it up for so many years that she's got nothing to be afraid of. She is open and honest about being trans when she meets people. There is such beauty in that honesty; I admire her because, although wisdom comes with age, I wouldn't have dealt with it nearly as well as she has dealt with everything.'

There will always be little things that people cannot get their heads around. Monica described how, if she has something on her mind that she wanted to discuss with Nicci, she would rather discuss it while responding to Nicci as a guy. Though Monica says she knows it is selfish on her part, she adds that she can 'feel' the difference between the two of them; she feels that Nicci is methodical and weighs up arguments and as a result will give her better advice as a guy. I do understand this, and I have no judgement of it. She is simply being honest about how she feels. For me, the issue is not that Nicci may be speaking to her as a guy or a girl—Nicci is speaking to her and giving advice as just one person and, as we know, any one person may be in various different frames of mind on any given day; so much so that any distinction can be very subtle. It doesn't mean that we are presenting as different people on different days.

Monica had a considerably less subtle reaction to Nicci coming out than other people we knew—something along the lines of: 'Oh my God, I've never seen a tranny before, I need to see your wardrobe!' I think this is funny and, knowing Monica, it is sort of endearing and simply a reflection of her personality. If we overlook the fundamental misunderstanding of her calling Nicci a 'tranny' rather than transgendered, I think Nicci took it all in good spirits. Hey, Rome wasn't built in a day.

'I'd never seen hip pads before. I begged to use her boob implants,' Monica added. 'She told me at a moment when we had time to explore it—to go through her make-up.' Monika shot me a cheeky wink.

I think her initial excitement was suddenly thinking that she had unknowingly acquired a gay friend

'It's every girl's dream to have a gay friend whose make-up you can use', she pointed out herself. 'All girls love having a gay friend they can go shopping with, and it's that kind of relationship where you can borrow their make-up and you know they are not going to make moves on you. You feel safe.'

Obviously, at the time of sitting with me while I interviewed her for this book, she had a changed her opinion on Nicci being gay—or at least, considered it a whole lot less likely!

Carol and her husband are probably the only people I know who are as understanding of Nicci as me, which is one of many reasons why I love being in their company. It is refreshing and easy for me—not that it is difficult with others as such, but I do notice the difference. This couple are essentially very good, decent and kind-hearted people. Carol has said that, when Nicci knocks on her and her husband's door, they are not bothered whether she is going to be dressed as a man or a woman.

'It has never bothered us,' said Carol. 'It's not about appearance—it is about who you are on the inside.'

Our discussion turned to the karaoke night when I had reminded Nicci she didn't have to dress as a woman because we were going somewhere trans friendly. 'No-one has ever been there before to say that to her', mused Carol. 'I think that is what Nicci appreciates about you; it doesn't matter to you whether she is male or female. And that is why Nicci is comfortable to be whoever she, or he, wants to be.'

I liked that Carol recognised the challenge faced by trans people coming out for the first time in a very different persona to how people had been used to their whole life. Other people had been accepting to the point of not questioning how hard it must be to walk out the door and face the world. As great as it is that they are so blasé about it, I find I am so akin with Carol in the sense that she just gets it—and at the very beginning, you need people around you who understand how hard it must be in order to really support you. On the other hand, it can be hard to find a balance—you don't want to mollycoddle the person. People pick up on vibes and if you make a big thing of it, others get the nervous signals and become nervous themselves.

While I knew the story from Nicci, I found it very moving when told by Carol. She was hosting a party and invited Nicci to come and be 'out' for the first time.

'Nicci was so nervous, she was literally shaking', Carol said. 'It would be hard for any trans person coming out—and it is important who you choose to come out to for the first time. It's about the people who are with you.

'It must have been, not so much terrifying, as more like hell. She was not just showing a different outward appearance—she was showing that there is a difference in her. Nicci was coming out to people who knew her as someone else. How are they going to react? She could only have known how they reacted to her as a man.

'I don't want to know what was going through Nicci's mind that day. I believe that she came out because she knew she had people around her who would support her.'

Carol understood that Nicci was not just coming out to Carol and her husband. She must have also been wondering and fretting about who else was going to be there. Not knowing anyone, how many people would she have to introduce herself to? Imagine how odd it would be to arrive at a party and, when you introduce yourself, present an entirely new name—and therefore, an entirely new persona—to the one you have presented your whole life.

'She was late and we knew that she must have been struggling with whether to come or not, prevaricating before coming because she was scared', Carol said. 'There were people there who did not know that she was not a woman.

'Nicci trusted us and we supported her that night—not only that, but we made sure that those who were going to be at our house were people that we believed were going to be supportive. We trusted them and we protected Nicci all the way through.'

I remember when Nicci first told me of this occasion; Carol was there the whole time, looking out for her. Not that it happened on many occasions, but when someone used 'he' instead of 'she', Carol gently corrected them.

'We had control, to some extent, of the surroundings that we put Nicci in for the first time—to make her feel secure and just as importantly, comfortable, in who she is.'

By the time I had met Nicci, that party was quite some way back in her past. Carol sharing her perspective helped hugely in putting a picture together for me. In my opinion, having that experience as Nicci's first outing did her the world of good in confidence building. Perhaps it made her think: 'This is not so bad. I can do this.' I said to Carol that Nicci has become so much more confident—but on some occasions, she still takes a second to pause before walking out of the door. But then, isn't that true of so many of us? We all have days where we feel less confident and don't feel like stepping outside.

Luckily, I have had nothing but warm, kind and loving comments from those close to Nicci about how accepting I am. They have said how I have had a positive influence in making her feel more comfortable with who she is.

Shout it From the Rooftops!

W hen you keep a secret, what is it that makes you keep it? What factors influence your decision not to tell? There could be several, but most commonly, we are afraid. We are afraid of embarrassing ourselves, hurting others, of possible repercussions and of the unknown.

When I interviewed Annie and asked her how her family would react if she came home with a partner who was transgendered she said: 'My dad would get the gun.' I wonder how many secrets you are holding that are likely to provoke this reaction if you confessed.

I think the biggest fear trans people have is the fear of losing family and being rejected. It is a real possibility. Trans relationships do break up and do result in divorce, which may result in losing the family home and reduced access to children; all this, at a time when someone has decided to come out and need more support and love than they have probably ever needed before in their lives.

Considering the risk a trans person takes, for all the reasons discussed, it is important that it is the individual's choice to 'come out'. If they do come out, it is up to them to choose when, to whom and to how many. No one else has the right to 'out' a trans person; each individual they confide in does not have the right to tell another soul.

The same is true for a trans partner. It is not just transgendered people who get outed—so was I, in my own way. You could say I was outed sporadically and having learned from Nicci's experience, I took the bull by the horns and came out guns blazing.

It happened that, shortly after I broke up with H, I met with my brother for drinks in a pub to confess the whirlwind of change that was happening in my life; how I had split up with my partner of 13 years and was now entering into a relationship with someone else. We talked for hours about all the reasons—many of them common to why any relationship ends—but not about the fact that H was a transvestite. At the end of my story, my brother asked me if there was anything else I wanted to tell him.

When someone asks you this question after you have a secret like the one I had kept for so long, your back rises like an animal bracing itself in a protective stance; your skin prickles and you feel instantly uncomfortable. You can usually pass this off as a guilty conscience. However, there was something in the way he had asked this that made me realise he knew H was a transvestite. In that moment, I was in a panic. After a few ridiculous rounds of questions like we were skirting round each other in a boxing ring, my brother confessed that he did in fact know that H was a transvestite.

This was a massive shock. I knew that, over the years, I had never given any indication. I had kept this secret very well hidden and I couldn't possibly imagine how he knew this. The very few people who did know had absolutely no connection to my brother and therefore had no occasion to have ever brought it to his attention. It was inconceivable to me that he should know.

My brother explained that, shortly after H and I broke up (and while he knew I was going to be at work) H paid a visit to my mum's house. By sheer coincidence, my brother happened to be visiting Mum. In the circumstances, this was a comfort to hear. In his defence, H was probably beside himself at the time and perhaps was not thinking about the consequences. Mum invited him in, offering all the usual pleasantries—though I am sure she must have been on her guard.

H sat in my mother's house and treated her hospitality like a church confession box—quite ironic, considering he had a deep hatred of religion and could not seem to pluck up the courage as to so much as set foot in any religious establishment. My brother relayed the conversation that was held when H went to see my mother.

'There is something I need to tell you,' H told the pair of them.

'No, you really don't have to tell us anything ...' Mum apparently replied quickly.

I don't think she could have possibly known what was coming, but she must have sensed it was something she would rather not hear—however, H had come on a mission and I don't think he had any intention of leaving until he had completed it. My brother said that Mum had been quite insistent that she did not want to know, but apparently not as insistent as H. Then he opened Pandora's Box and told my mum and brother that he was transvestite.

When I heard about this, I was livid, incensed. I felt cheated, angry and a whole host of other emotions, none of which were pleasant, I can assure you. This was for so many reasons; not only had he shown no respect for my mum's wish not to have this bombshell dropped on her, but he had also gone behind my back and told my family, though I had kept his secret for 13 years! That is a very long time to respect someone else's secret, when there were times I did need someone else to talk to about it. How dare he, how dare he? Even more offensively, I had not yet had the opportunity to even tell my brother that H and I had split up, so he dropped that bombshell as well, robbing me of the opportunity of telling my own brother something so important.

I was not ready to tell my family about Nicci yet; I wanted to choose the time and place carefully. Yet, in some ways (as Nicci later pointed out), this confession had paved the way of the future of my and Nicci's relationship. It must have planted a seed which eventually grew into fruition. I could think that this might have been the motivation behind H's actions—aside from purging himself—but I will never know.

I left that drink with my brother agreeing that I was not ready to speak with Mum about what had been reported to me so soon. When I next saw her, we naturally discussed how our conversation had gone; how it went, telling my brother that I had split up with H. She asked me the same dynamite question: 'Is there anything else you want to talk about?' This time I simply said no.

I should have learnt from Nicci's experience earlier. I think, over time, a mother's instinct got the better of my mum. I can't remember the specifics but she acquired, shall we say, enough information to put two and two together. Eventually, I knew that she had enough suspicion to know that Nicci was (in her words) 'the same as H'. The understanding that Nicci is not on the same place on the spectrum as H came later, but initially there was an almighty row, mostly shouting on my part from blind anger that she had invaded my privacy to build her case of evidence. My behaviour was ugly and I now understand her reasoning much better.

Carol asked me what kind of support network H had around him when I relayed this story to her. I replied honestly that I was the only person in his support network. Carol thought for a moment.

'For H, you were not enough; you were just one, against millions.' Carol said, which I thought was a very good point. Well, Nicci regularly recognises me as one in a million, but she sees this as a very positive thing—such is the difference in attitude.

The point is everyone has a right to 'come out' when they are ready and in the way they choose. This is a right in itself, but also one has to consider that the reactions of others and their level of (dis)comfort can be so varied. Since clearing things up with my mother, I can say that we have a better relationship now than we have ever had in adulthood, which is both a relief and a major positive, as we can now just enjoy each others' company.

So how did Nicci come out? Well, she didn't have a lot of choice, as it happened. She was 'outed', in a negative and vindictive way—yet I think she would agree with me when I say that it is probably the best thing that ever happened in her life; the turning point. Nicci had the experience of coming out in her own time taken from her when she was outed at work.

She tells the story better than me; in fact, she has told it probably one hundred times to audiences all over the country, as part of her stand-up comedy routine. She has told it to educate others in transgendered awareness workshops, she has delivered it at conferences and at evening seminars. You get the picture. I will try and do it justice.

It goes something like this: she was working at a college at the time and was testing the water when it came to telling people about being transgender. She thought she could trust her line manager and had chatted a few times to her about it. This woman never indicated that she had a problem with it, or was uncomfortable with it in any way. Nicci then went on holiday for a few weeks and when she got home, there was a letter informing her that she should not return to work as normal, but should attend a meeting with the principal and her manager on a specific given date. Naturally, Nicci was worried and perturbed by what the issue could possibly be.

Nicci couldn't have possibly imagined what was about to come—that she would be hit with a sledgehammer blow. She arrived at the meeting and was told that they knew she was transgendered. They proceeded to try and pin non-existent performance issues on to this. It is impossible to know what it must feel like to have your deepest secret laid out before you by a panel at work when you thought that no one knew—that the one person you confided in betrayed you in the most destructive way possible.

The result was two-fold. First, the line manager that outed Nicci was hauled over the coals for her unjustified actions and she lost her job. Secondly, Nicci spent a week locked in her room (she was flat sharing at the time), sobbing her heart out. If it were me, I would be thinking that my world had ended. For a week she didn't eat and didn't sleep—she just cried and cried.

She jokes now that this was a great way to drop a dress size, but at that time she naturally did a lot of serious soul-searching, thinking about her future. As her strength grew, she started making some decisions and became bold. She vowed that she would never let anyone 'out' her again. The only way to do that was come out to everyone; the rest of her colleagues at the college, her family and her friends. This is where, as I see it, Nicci was born. It was the making of her.

The college were amazing at supporting her. So much so, in fact, that is why they invited her to present four sessions to over 200 members of staff at the diversity day I have previously mentioned. It was the first time she had gone to work dressed as a woman and the reception was phenomenal.

During the diversity day, the different sessions were run in different lecture halls and people moved around them throughout the day, choosing which they wished to attend in a round-robin style. By the afternoon, our sessions were packed to the rafters; gossip had spread like wild fire that Nicci's presentation was the best and everyone wanted to come. I am sure there was a curiosity factor about the issue of transgender—which was great, because it gave us the opportunity to educate many more people.

This was the beginning of Nicci realising that, to her, being trans meant more than just being out and open; she also had a message to give to the world, a need to educate others and to help it become more accepted. She could help create understanding, acceptance and integration for all trans women in society.

After the incident with H and my mum, I then followed Nicci's example and decided no one else would find out about Nicci in such an uncontrollable manner; I would prevent this by making sure I was the one telling everyone about it. Although it can't possibly be on the same scale as a trans person coming out, there was something incredibly liberating about sharing a secret which, in reality, I had held for over 13 years. Though I was with Nicci, I had also been with someone on the trans spectrum for the whole time I had been with H. After so long, it was freeing to allow this fact to become part of everyday conversations.

Monica asked me if I was relieved after my parents knew about Nicci. Indeed, it was a huge relief because the alternative would be pretending that Nicci was someone else—and also because I had kept quiet for so many years with H. Of course, staying quiet about Nicci for a while was not on the same scale, but it felt longer than it was—like the 'bottleneck of time' trans people experience when they come out. Completely wearing your heart on your sleeve gives new colour to your whole life; I began to fall in love with this newfound defiance. I found it was giving me a richer, fuller experience to all my relationships.

As for Nicci, she has battled hard to be in a situation where she feels in control of her own life, and it has been on one hell of journey— like the journey of a single salmon swimming against the fierce current in order to breed. That is how I see Nicci's journey of coming out; she had to start again from the beginning, to shape her life as the person that she is rather than the person she had pretended to be for 39 years. It takes huge strength of character and power of will to keep fighting against the tide. This part of her impresses me—this part of many trans women—hence why I am always surprised whenever Nicci has moments of weakness and insecurity (though we all do). I bring her back and remind her of what she is fighting for.

I have already said that it is fundamental to Nicci's character that she does not deny her true self. She has said, at points, that there has always been some part of her that she has not addressed, and has always felt that there is a certain purpose she is supposed to fulfil. For the majority of her life, she has not really known what this is; it has always been just a feeling. This may sound a little corny depending on your view, but from my observation throughout her journey of coming out, this feeling has progressed in strength and gained momentum.

It is my perspective that this became clearer to her at the end of that day at the College, when she delivered the transgendered session for the diversity day. We came home to her flat and flopped, exhausted (due to the lack of sleep that comes from preparing for such a hectic weekend) but exhilarated. I think the gravity of what Nicci had achieved was beginning to sink in; she spoke seven simple words in the contented silence, which in retrospect, I think were a momentous milestone. She said: 'This is what I should be doing.' I think this was the beginning of her next journey—her wanting to present to an audience.

If even her close friends didn't really understand transgender, then I think in that moment she realised she had a duty to educate others—this is what she had perhaps felt she needed to do all her life; her calling or vocation, you could say. Nicci understands, now more than ever, that her talent and passion is having a profound effect on her audience. This is particularly evident when you are there in the moment, listening to her speak.

Her journey now is finding and utilising every method she can in order to educate others on transgender; what it is and how it affects her. She has worked with GIRES (Gender Identity Research and Education Society) and an educational organisation called LSIS to deliver workshops on transgender across the county. She has spoken at conferences, delivered at evening inspirational talks and she is also a talented stand-up comedian. When she has an audience at her fingertips, her message is always simple yet powerful, because it is her story. Listeners find it moving, humbling, humorous and, I think, a unique experience, insomuch as they have never been exposed to the subject of transgender in the way that Nicci shares it.

Nicci is becoming her own brand—something we might all benefit from doing. I would be proud of her for just standing tall and walking out into the world every day, perhaps sometimes afraid, but defiant nevertheless. I am immensely proud of her for having courage where so many others would not; to be trans and 'out', just as I am proud of everyone we know and love, trans friends and acquaintances. For every trans girl in the world who I haven't met, I salute you—each and every one of you—for the courage of conviction. How many of us can honestly say we have this? I think that we all have lessons to learn from these women. In addition to this, Nicci is not just living her everyday life; she is sharing it with whoever will listen. She is dedicating herself to teaching, whether by way of humour, education or compassion. It is an honour to know her, let alone love her and be her partner.

A Better Life

I think it would be fair to say that both Nicci and I have come a long way. I remember back to that time in the spa, contemplating my situation with H—it wasn't just him, but every area of my life was turned over tentatively, like a stone in the earth. With every turn, I grew less hesitant of what I might find underneath each stone. I learned not to care about the dirt or the worms in my mind; the unpleasant realisations I was uncovering. As I came to a conclusion for each problem, I felt stronger. The world I lived in then, so choked up with the expectations from all the people I shared it with, was beginning to look so unreal. I stood back from it and viewed it through completely selfish eyes.

The prospect of leaving was scary at first; I was lost, for a short while, without the routine of being two people as one unit. Yet, I was amazed at how quickly my strength grew, and how free I began to feel. I still feel that same freedom, even though I am in a relationship and this is what makes my current one healthy. I feel like me, not a shadow of myself. I have had to experience many things, some big and some small, to get to this point.

There was a moment during my period in no-man's-land—between my old life and new life—that was so powerful I would like to share it with you. An unlikely event; an away-day training session at my old work. My job was field-based, and this event was away from home and the team were staying in a hotel in Birmingham. HR led a particular activity in the morning of the first day, which plagued me for the next two days and may have contributed to a drink too many in the bar that evening. I will describe it as best I can remember it, or the essence of it at least, as it was virtually life-changing for me. It involved boxes ironically—quite literally.

The woman leading the activity was also called Laura. She had used duct tape to mark out a large square on the floor. Within the square, she had divided the space into four. In the top left box the word 'impossible' was marked out in tape, the top right box was marked 'possible', the bottom left box marked 'I can achieve anything' and the last box was empty. She started the activity by standing in the 'impossible' box and explained that, when you are faced with a big task or new project, at first it may seem impossible. You might stress, worry and wonder how you are ever going to achieve it. It feels 'impossible'.

She then stepped into the 'possible' box and explained that, as you get stuck into the work or start to tackle the issue, you relax a little and see that it is not impossible and you can achieve the task. She then stepped into the 'I can achieve anything' box, which is when you are high on coming to the end of the project. The sky is your limit; your skills know no bounds.

Stepping into the empty box, she explained that in reality, throughout there will be times when you are in a spin and moving rapidly from each box in a cycle. It is about recognising which box you are in, to keep you focused.

Laura went on to talk about the influence of others, occasionally stepping in and out of the boxes as she talked. She said that we could also recognise when others are in the different boxes and when you can help them or when they are a hindrance to you. As a group, we talked about the ways in which we could help those who are a hindrance move into a more positive box.

'What if you have done all you can to support the person in the "impossible" box,' Laura asked, 'and they are clearly never going to be moved? In fact, you recognise that they are dragging you down.'

A colleague gave an example of her relationship with a friend. She said the end result was that this person was pulling her down so much that she made the conscious decision, although difficult, to cut this person out of her life.

Laura summarised that the activity was about understanding that we all operate by moving around the boxes. This is never going to change because it is human nature but consciously being aware of how we operate can help. She agreed that, sometimes, we can support someone as much as possible—but there has to come a time when they help themselves move into the more positive boxes and if they are not willing to do this, it can mean deciding to abandon the relationship or else accepting that this person will continue to make you operate from a negative working space if you let them.

It is typical motivational-speech material, but it really did hit me like a bolt of lightning. I sat there in that crowd of my colleagues and thought 'That is my relationship. H is constantly in that "impossible" box, and I have moved around the other boxes but am forced to keep coming back. I have got to abandon the relationship for my own preservation.' I don't mind telling you, readers, that thought put me right in the 'impossible' box!

Several months later, when I had broken up with H, I told Laura the effect this exercise had on me was to help me decide to split up with my partner—and that it should come with a warning. I gave her my express permission that I would like her to tell other delegates my story when she runs this activity in future—in fact, I stressed that I wanted her to. After the initial shock, she was pleased it had had such a powerful and positive life-changing effect on me.

These events in our lives are only as powerful as the worth and meaning we give them. It is what you decide to do about them that helps you create the person you want to be, and encourages you really to think of the world as your oyster. In case you couldn't tell, ever since this 'event', I mostly operate from the 'I can achieve anything' box. There are no limits to me living my dreams—you are reading one of them.

You create yourself from your experiences. Some experiences come to you, but only by being in control of them do they shape who you are. You must review and analyse your past encounters.

At moments of great decision, it is your heart, your soul, your gut instinct, your true desire and that bolt of lightning—however impulsive or dramatic it may seem—that should drive the decisions you make. These are your truth; these are what is real, and it is important not to ignore them. You cannot influence the truth that belongs to others, or move them out of their comfort zone of 'impossible'.

Our minds are incredibly powerful tools and can play tricks on us. The negatives can cripple our ability to make decisions. Learn to recognise what thoughts are actually excuses. Are we hiding behind the negatives because they are safe and cosy—do we wrap ourselves in them like a warm blanket and revel in the smokescreen they provide in our darkest moments?

I didn't want to be alone and I didn't think I could find someone else. Looking back on it now, this is quite tragic, but I now feel so far removed from who that woman was. Whoever she was, she was not me. It is frightening that a person can get to this stage for fear of changing anything. I did not behave in what I consider was a healthy way for my needs.

I can't help think that many of you reading this can see something of yourself in my example, in a relationship you have been in or are in. I urge you not to repeat my mistakes; deal with concerns about your relationship head on and in an amicable a way as possible. Don't stick you head in the sand, hoping that eventually a sand storm will come and blow your troubles away. I urge you to question, as I did. Fear stops ourselves and others living the lives we deserve to live. Being a part of the crowd will lead you to a life that is far removed from the one you want.

That said, I have no regrets; regrets are pointless and I would not be where I am now if I had taken a different path. I would not be the person I am today if I had made different decisions.

When you find something your heart desires, don't necessarily accept the initial denial your 'impossible' box gives you; question how easily you are willing to give it up. I moved on because I could see that staying where I was, everything was going to be 'impossible'. What was really impossible was giving up on Nicci. I believed this without doubt in my heart, no rhyme or reason involved. I knew that if I chose to end my relationship with H, there was nothing I couldn't achieve and I would have a life that would be one hell of a journey. I realised life is about the journey, not the destination.

Nicci is my Princess and I am her Angel. She believes that my views are so unique that she wonders where on earth I came from; she concluded that perhaps I didn't come from Earth but by some other miracle. Occasionally she can be 'having a moment' (as we call it between us) because she cannot believe that she has found someone who thinks the way I do about her being trans and has the attitude, acceptance and encouragement that I do—as a partner of a trans person. I like to think that perhaps together we are a force to be reckoned with.

I am not in her shadow by any means; Nicci encourages my journey much as I encourage hers and I, too, am on a mission to share my passion in a way that others can understand. Hey, what do you think you are reading right now? Just as much as I believe in trans people's rights to simply be themselves, I believe it is everyone's right to be free from the constraints and burdens placed on us. We all have the right to be free to express who we are, using our outward appearance, without encountering discrimination.

I guess the person you are deep down is never very far from you. I opened Pandora's Box because making one big change seemed to ricochet through other areas of my life and in as little as the first six months of having left the relationship, I discovered a fundamental lesson, which I would like you to take away with you, because it could serve us all well. It goes thus: if you knew with confidence that you could handle anything life could throw at you (and realistically as humans, we can because very often we have to) then you start to lose the fear that rules your life. This makes you stronger, and the earlier in life you can learn—and more importantly, experience—this lesson, the better.

The difference between my relationship with Nicci and past relationships is me. I am a stronger person for knowing that my relationship is not the be-all and end-all. There would be life after Nicci for me, if something were to happen. Of course, I would be devastated; I would be heart-broken but intellectually I would know that, eventually, I would somehow move on because I would not have become so much a part of her that I would not be able to function without her. The same is true vice versa; I am my own, unique being and I share my life with another unique being.

The past is important, as one of my favourite quotes powerfully illustrates, particularly as it comes from the father of Anne Frank—Otto. It goes: 'Without the past, we have no future.' It is absolutely true—our past shapes who we are every single day.

The past is only wasted if we don't learn from it.

The gift of perspective has made me see what is really important in life is fighting for the right simply to be yourself. This counts for all of us, but particularly in the context of trans people. Considering the huge undertaking this is for many trans people, it would be churlish for me not to have reviewed myself in the process and come to the conclusion of how very lucky indeed I am. I no longer chastise myself for not being the perfect woman that the media heavily encourages women to be. I am not apologising for my flaws, amending them or curbing them so that they are more palatable for those around me. It is a relief, it is refreshing; and once grey clouds of self-doubt that once hung over you are allowed to vaporise into the distant past, the result is that you can actually enjoy life fully, without inhibition.

I believe only you can drive your own destiny. I believe that life, in all its colour, its pain, joy and variety, is beautiful. I have an eclectic taste in everything; music, books, films and, most importantly, friends. Life is not a box of chocolates; you choose what you are going to get and it doesn't fall into your lap. You have to work hard and fight for what you want and for those you love.

I am very open minded, I am accepting of others' uniqueness; I embrace difference. I would never deny anyone their right to be themselves, completely. When I love, I love passionately, whatever the passion or whoever the friend or lover.

I am less afraid; I don't let fear prevent me from facing things that are uncomfortable, hearing the truth, however difficult. I am not afraid to step out into public with my transgendered partner and tell the world I love her. I am not afraid to stand up for any transgendered person and teach others to understand.

I am proud of myself for always trying to stand up for what is right, for making uncomfortably difficult decisions, for being dyslexic and yet gaining a degree and publishing a book. I am proud of my partner's bravery to be different and unapologetic for who she is. I am proud of her as a beautiful person. I am proud of my friends and family, my parents and brother, full stop; but in particular for being so cool about Nicci being transgendered.

Life is about fun and joy and finding laughter everywhere, even in the bleakest situations.

Lastly, I am a richer person, with richer experiences, who has been lucky enough to have met brave, admirable, genuine people and to have experienced the opportunities and opinions meeting them has rewarded me with. I am lucky that this has strengthened all my existing relationships.

I am unapologetic for who I am, for what I believe in, and for this gushing end.

Appendix:
♡ *Here comes the science bit …*

This helpful list of terminology has been produced by GIRES (Gender Identity Research and Education Society) and is used with their kind permission.

Terminology in the 'transgender' field is varied and constantly shifting as our understanding and perceptions of gender variant conditions changes. The concept of a 'normal' gender expression associated with a binary man/woman paradigm is, in itself, questionable. In addition, in writing such a list of definitions there is a risk of merely creating further stereotypes. People have the right to self-identify, and many people, especially among the young, now see themselves as falling outside the gender tick-boxes, and they may use terms such as pan-gender, poly-gender, neutrois, third gender, gender queer and, occasionally, non-gendered. All these fall outside the typical gender tick-boxes, and may denote varying, or fluctuating gender experiences, or a complete rejection of the concept of gender.

Gender identity

Gender identity describes the psychological identification of oneself, usually as a boy/man or as a girl/woman. There is a presumption that this sense of identity will evolve along binary lines and be consistent with the sex appearance. However, not everyone will wish to be constrained by that binary form of categorization. Some people experience a gender identity that is completely inconsistent with their sex appearance, or may be neutral, or may embrace aspects of both man and woman.

Sex

Sex refers to the male/female physical development—the phenotype. In an infant, the sex is judged entirely on the genital appearance at birth. Other phenotypic factors such as karyotype (chromosomal configuration) are seldom tested unless a genital anomaly is present. There is a presumption that an apparently male infant will identify as a boy, and vice versa.

Gender role

The gender role is the social role—the interaction with others which both gives expression to the inner gender identity and reinforces it. Despite the greater gender equality in modern Western culture in terms of: the subjects studied in school and at university; the choice of friends; work and domestic arrangements; dress and leisure pursuits, there is still a presumption of conformity with society's 'rules' about what is appropriate for a man or a woman, a boy or a girl, especially in terms of appearance. A significant departure from stereotypical gender expression often causes anxiety and discomfort in those who witness it.

Gender variance/gender dysphoria/gender nonconformity

It is now understood that the innate gender identity, although powerfully influenced by the sex of the genitalia and the gender of rearing, is not determined by these factors. There is evidence that sex differentiation of the brain may be inconsistent with other sex characteristics, resulting in individuals dressing and/or behaving in a way which is perceived by others as being outside cultural gender norms; these unusual gender expressions may be described as gender variance, or gender nonconformity. Not everyone who is gender nonconforming experiences personal discomfort. However, where conforming with society's norms causes a persistent personal discomfort, this may be described as gender dysphoria. In many, this includes some level of disgust with the phenotype, since this contradicts the inner sense of gender identity. Gender dysphoria is now used in preference to the terms gender identity disorder and transsexualism. The latter terms imply a diagnosis of pathology and are currently being replaced by gender dysphoria or gender incongruence in medical literature (2012), but will still appear in some documents. The neutral terms, gender variance or gender nonconforming, denote that departures from stereotypical gender experience and expression are part of a natural, albeit unusual, human development.

Transsexualism

Gender variance may be experienced to a degree that medical intervention is sometimes necessary, and may include hormone therapy and surgical procedures to change the appearance and improve personal comfort. Often these treatments are associated with a permanent transition to a gender role that accords with the gender identity, thus alleviating much or all of the discomfort. At this level of intensity, the condition is still known as transsexualism in some medical environments, but it is under review and the term may eventually be replaced in newer medical literature. A transsexual person, would be someone who intends to undergo, is undergoing or has undergone gender reassignment. The word 'transsexual' should be used as an adjective, not a noun. It is, therefore, not appropriate to refer to an individual as 'a transsexual', or to transsexual people, as 'transsexuals'; the abbreviation 'tranny' is also unacceptable.

Transition

Transition is the term used to describe the permanent change of gender role to one that is congruent with the gender identity. This change affects all spheres of life: family and work environments, leisure pursuits and in society generally. A few people make this change overnight, but many arrive at the point of full-time gender role changes, after months or even years of intermittent gender role change. The term 'affirmed' gender, is now becoming more common in describing the post-transition gender.

Gender confirmation treatment

Those transitioning permanently usually have gender confirmation treatment that includes hormone therapy and sometimes surgery to bring the sex characteristics of the body more in line with the gender identity. Such surgery is sometimes referred to as gender (or sex) reassignment surgery. The term 'sex change' is not considered appropriate or polite.

Transgender

Transgenderism has had different meanings over time, and in different societies. Currently, it is used as an inclusive term describing all those whose gender expression falls outside the typical gender norms; for example, those who cross-dress intermittently for a variety of reasons including erotic factors (also referred to as transvestism), as well as those who live continuously outside gender norms, sometimes with, and sometimes without, medical intervention. There is a growing acknowledgement that although there is a great deal of difference between say, a drag artist and a transsexual person, there are nonetheless areas in the transgender field where the distinctions are more blurred; for example, someone who cross-dresses intermittently for some years, may later transition fully to the opposite role.

Trans men and trans women

The expression 'trans' is often used synonymously with 'transgender' in its broadest sense. However, sometimes its use is specific; for instance, those born with female appearance but identifying as men may be referred to as 'trans men'; and those born with male appearance but identifying as women may be referred to as 'trans women'. Many trans people, having transitioned permanently, prefer to be regarded as ordinary men and women. In these cases, where it becomes essential to refer to their pre-transition status, the phrase 'woman (or man) of transsexual history' may be used.

Intersex conditions

There are a number of intersex conditions (recently renamed Disorders of Sex Development) which may lead the individuals born with them to experience some inconsistency between their gender identity, and the gender role assigned at birth. Inconsistencies in development may be associated with atypical sex chromosomes such as Klinefelter syndrome (XXY), Jacob's syndrome (XYY), or other genetic anomalies, such as Androgen Insensitivity Syndrome or Congenital Adrenal Hyperplasia in which unusual hormone levels, or hormone responses, are present. These may lead, for instance, to physical genital anomalies.

Sexual orientation

Sexual orientation is a separate issue from gender identity. Sexual orientation is associated with the sexual attraction between one person and another. This is quite different from the internal knowledge of one's own identity. Trans people may be gay, straight, bisexual or, occasionally, asexual. Their sexual relationships may remain the same through the transition process, or they may change. So a person who is living as a man, and is in a heterosexual relationship with a woman may, having transitioned to live as a woman, continue to be attracted to women and seek a lesbian relationship—or—may be attracted to men, and therefore seek a heterosexual relationship with a man. Sometimes trans people make lasting relationships with other trans people, so the possibilities are many and varied, and do not necessarily fit comfortably into typical categorisations of sexual behaviours.

Gender Recognition Certificate (GRC)

In 2004 the Gender Recognition Act was passed, and it became effective in 2005. Those trans people who have undergone a permanent change of gender role may endorse their new gender status by obtaining legal recognition in the form of a GRC. Those whose birth was registered in the UK are then entitled to a new birth certificate registered under the changed name and title. Genital surgery is not a pre-requisite. People with a GRC have, 'for all purposes', the gender status that is congruent with the gender identity.

Cisgender

Those who are cisgender have little or no discordance between their gender identity and their gender role or sex characteristics. These factors are well aligned in a cisgendered person. Trans people who have completed transition to the point that they are comfortable, may then be regarded as cisgender.

© Gender Identity Research and Education Society (GIRES)

www.gires.org.uk

Also from Bramley Press

Grrl Alex: A personal journey to a transgender identity

Alex Drummond

A moving, emotional and true story.

From the moment of our birth, our gender is assigned to us. But what if the grown-ups got it wrong—what if you feel you really should be in the other group? This is not an easy equation for a young child to figure, especially when certain behaviours that seem natural get you into mega trouble: playing with the 'wrong toys', wanting to wear 'the wrong clothes', doing stuff that only applies to 'the opposite sex'.

The possibility of embracing transgender as a legitimate identity is a relatively new phenomenon, and what this book achieves in straightforward and engaging language is to combine formal academic research with a deeply moving personal narrative, to give the reader an insight into the world of a person who came to accept and embrace a transgender identity.

Realisations

Andie Davidson

The transgender experience is highly diverse, and no writing can truly encompass it. At the same time, prose narrative can leave you outside the reality, always as an observer. This collection of poetry reflects the realisation – the 'real I' discovery – of coming to terms with being transgender, and how this journey into self impacts on family, friends and the wider world. Each section is prefaced by a short introduction that explains some of the transgender issues for the less familiar reader.
A Sense of gender; Facing change; Appearances; Social awareness; It's personal! The shock; Family acceptance; Finding resolution.

www.bramleypress.co.uk welcomes good new trans authors